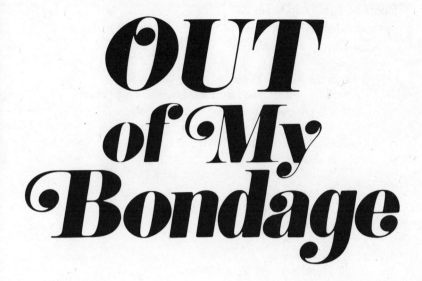

OUT of My Bondage

Marion B. West

D0041318

BROADMAN PRESS
Nashville, Tennessee

For my husband—Jerry
　my children—Julie, Jennifer, Jeremy, and Jon
　my mother—Jewette

　　and the Scribe Tribe, Atlanta, Georgia
　　without whose love, encouragement, and prayers
　　this book could not have been written.
　　　Cec and Shirley Murphey
　　　Charlotte Smith Allen
　　　Suzanne Stewart
　　　Joyce McKennon and Mac McKennon (deceased)
　　　Martin Burks
　　　Mary Jepson
　　　Rosemary Jones
　　　John Allen
　　　Mike Keedy
　　　Markham and Eddie Berry
　　　Ovid Campbell
　　　Venera Weldon
　　　Dartha Whitis

　　And Evelyn Campbell, who read each word
　　with amazing patience and determination.

© Copyright 1976 • Broadman Press
All rights reserved
4282-42 (BRP edition)
4251-44 (trade edition)
ISBN: 0-8054-5144-7

Dewey Decimal Classification: 301.427
Subject headings: MARRIAGE//WOMAN//FAMILY
Library of Congress Catalog Card Number: 76-5297
Printed in the United States of America

Contents

Preface

As surely as a baby grows and its mother becomes aware of the growth, this book has grown inside me. I didn't plan it, and I often ignored it. But that didn't stop the growth.

As the book grew I insisted I couldn't give it birth. Many times I thought the book had been aborted, and I felt relief.

But it grew and was strong. And the day came that this book asked to be born. And when that time came I was glad I had been chosen to be the mother. I wanted the book to live.

It had to live!

God was in its conception and birth.

Out Of My Bondage was written for those who love the Lord and for those who have wondered about loving him. If you come one step closer to him through reading this book, then it was written especially for you.

Out of my bondage, sorrow, and night,

Jesus, I come, Jesus, I come;

Into thy freedom, gladness, and light,

Jesus, I come to thee;

Out of my sickness into thy health,

Out of my want and into thy wealth,

Out of my sin and into thyself,

Jesus, I come to thee.

WILLIAM T. SLEEPER

Scripture quotations marked TLB are from *The Living Bible, Paraphrased* (Wheaton: Tyndale House Publishers, 1971) and are used by permission.

1

I'm Not Going to Make It, God

I stood in my backyard, holding the two overflowing sacks of garbage. I held them tightly, not wanting to dump them into the trash container. Then I would *have* to go back into the house.

I felt like part of the garbage . . . and almost wished I could jump in with it and have the lid placed back on the can.

The coldness of the night was delicious. I shivered and inhaled deeply. For just a few moments I was alone. I savored the privacy.

I didn't want to go back in there . . . to a house with four children. In spite of a good husband and a nice home, I felt like a failure. Two girls and twin boys—especially the toddling twins—were more than I could cope with. Almost every day was a nightmare that I cried and screamed my way through.

Each day loomed ahead like an eternity; I resented the demanding babies and hated myself for it. I'd always known what I wanted to be when I grew up—a mother! And now I felt I couldn't take it one day at a time anymore. I was too tired. I hadn't known motherhood would involve every minute of every day—and still the children would continue demanding more. I didn't have any more to give.

I liked things neat and orderly and on schedule. As an only child, I was used to having privacy. Now I couldn't have my own Scotch tape or pencils. My drawers were rambled through . . . and I couldn't, even after twelve years of marriage, get used to picking up after everyone.

The twins were unusually active and destructive. Two ladies from the church stopped by one day. I had been absent from services for quite a while. The women had just come from the beauty shop. Maids were cleaning their homes. Their children were almost grown. Now my friends were going shopping and out to lunch. But they had come by to tell me they missed me at church. They wanted to know why I hadn't been coming.

Old blankets covered the brick hearth where Jon and Jeremy, not yet a year old, often fell. They had removed the tubes from the television. Curtains were missing from the den because they had pulled down both the curtains and the rods. We had moved so many things and so much furniture out, there was an echo in the room as we talked. All their toys were scattered across the floor, along with empty cereal boxes. Dirty diapers were stacked in the bathroom.

It was so good to have adults to talk with, but as soon as we sat down the boys crawled into the fireplace and began reaching up the chimney. I snatched both of them, holding one between my knees and the other in my arms. They arched their backs and screamed for freedom.

The ladies' visit lasted five minutes. "How do you stand it?" one of them asked in open honesty as they were leaving.

"I'd go crazy," the other laughed.

They encouraged me to come back to church. As I watched them drive away, tears slid down my face. *I can't stand it either. I am going crazy!*

As I looked at the mess I would live with all day I wondered: "How can I be the same person who just a few years ago never had a thing out of place?"

My fastidiousness once caused my mother to sleep on top of the spread when she spent the night with us. I questioned, "Why in the world aren't you under the cover?"

She laughed, "I knew you had the bed made a certain way and that I couldn't remake it." I laughed, too, never seeing how pathetic her statement was.

Now I was becoming chilled as I stood in my dark backyard and looked at lights in the neighborhood. *I'm failing. How can I fail at something as important as motherhood. I can't fail, and I don't know how to succeed. I'm caught in the middle. I just want out.*

I shut my eyes for a moment and the familiar tears slid down my cold cheeks. *I have to go back inside. That's my world.* I pictured my kitchen; supper dishes to be washed. Two highchairs caked in sticky crumbs and spilled tea and a floor littered with gummy food awaited me.

In the den there were books, toys, cookie crumbs, pots and pans, torn magazines, everyone's shoes. When these were gathered up, a mountain of diapers waited to be folded. Jon and Jeremy must be bathed and forced into pajamas. They would struggle, making a game out of it. Julie and Jennifer would be waiting for Jerry to help them with their math.

A little part of me still cried out silently, "Jerry, please let's talk in a room where there isn't a thing that looks childlike." But most of me insisted, "What's the use? By the time all the children are satisfied and in bed, I will have fallen across my bed asleep in my clothes, and Jerry will be unable to awaken me."

I loved sleep. It relieved me of all responsibility of doing anything for anyone. But it only lasted for a short time. I'd learned to hate morning. Everybody wanted something at the same time. Wet, hungry, destructive, jabbering twins to satisfy—all day long.

Almost numb from the cold, I still delayed going back into the house. Jerry had offered to take the garbage out tonight. I had wanted to smile and say, "Thanks, love." Instead I had screamed: "No, you go out every day. It's my turn. Give it to me. Is the world still out there?"

Still holding the garbage, I looked up at the sky. It was beautiful. I hadn't appreciated beauty in so long. But I had four beautiful children. There's Orion—just like it used to be when I was a little girl and my girl friend and I laid out on a quilt to watch falling stars.

Was there really ever a time when I had all the freedom I wanted and when I wasn't tired?

I sobbed out loud. There were no children to watch me. I wasn't used to privacy. Looking up at the stars and sky I realized with absolute certainty something I'd known for a long time. There's a God all right. He exists.

9

He's just forgotten about me. If only I could get his attention. How does one get God's attention? Does everyone but me who goes to church have something I've missed?

I was going down for the third time, and I wanted to be pulled back up to happiness. I wanted to smile again . . . at my husband . . . my children . . . and myself.

Still looking at the sky and hoping desperately that he was listening, I said aloud, "I'm not going to make, God."

2

The Holy Spirit in the Midst of Crumbs

Back in the house things were exactly as I had expected. Mutely I did all that must be done, moving rapidly, to hasten the time I could go to bed and sleep. As I picked up strewn items in the den, I kept thinking about my prayer.

I knew in my heart my prayer meant more than what I had said aloud. I was saying, *I can't do it. Look down. See me. Help me. I desperately need you, God.*

Prayer wasn't foreign to me. As a small child I had prayed and in my teen years, too—when things got bad enough. My prayers were requests. I knew nothing of praising God or of listening to him. Now that I think back I realize I didn't believe it was right, somehow, to go to God with anything but a tremendous problem.

I had accepted Christ when I was a child of nine. I believed Jesus was God's Son, and I accepted all I understood. The water in the pool at First Baptist Church in Elberton, Georgia, had been warmed, and I wore a white robe. I felt very special—even with my hair wet and dripping onto my dress afterwards.

But no one told me about daily trust. No one told me of daily surrender. I trusted Jesus to save me after death, but no one made it clear He would save me from daily problems and fears.

Mine had piled up into a dense forest in which I was lost. In

10

my confusion and desperation I began to wonder if it were possible for God to help me overcome the panicky feelings I had. I could try. I didn't know anything else to do.

In the morning things were no better. I awoke with an accusing thought: God doesn't care about you.

Jerry's voice was sharp. "Marion, the boys are out of their beds and going out the door. Hurry! Get up!"

"I'm not going to get up anymore."

"Don't be funny. I'm almost late for work. Look! They're out in the yard in their pajamas. They're going to turn over the birdbath!"

"I don't care. I'm not getting up."

Jerry ran out the door with only one shoe on. I looked out the window, sitting up in bed. I saw him returning to the house with a laughing boy under each arm. Jerry wasn't laughing.

I desperately wanted *him* to have to care for them for days and days. And it should rain every day.

I pulled the cover over my head. I had never refused to get up before. It both pleased and frightened me. *Maybe now Jerry will realize I can't cope and send me somewhere. It won't be my decision. Or maybe, surely, he'll stay home today.*

He stood at the foot of the bed. "I have to go to work, Marion. The husband goes to work, and the mother cares for the children." He dumped the boys onto the bed with me. I began crying.

When I heard the door slam, I knew he'd gone to work on schedule. The shock of it stopped my crying. He either didn't care about us or he was the cleverest man alive.

Jeremy brought a box of cereal to the bed, leaving a trail behind him. "Yum, yum, Mama." I heard the refrigerator door open and knew Jon was eating whatever he found—spilling most of it.

Wearily, I picked Jeremy up and went into the kitchen. As I passed the girls' room, I noticed they had made their beds as best they could. I had heard Julie, the fourth grader, helping Jennifer, who was in the second grade, select what to wear. Then she reminded her to get her lunch money. They had already left on the school bus. I started crying again, thinking of how little time or energy I had for them.

11

As I put the boys in their high chairs I thought, *I can do it one more time—just today—then something different will happen. Just do it today. It won't be like this much longer.*

While they ate and threw food on the floor, I sat at the table watching them. My obduracy gave way to fright of the day that loomed ahead.

I'm scared and unhappy, God, and tired. I need to talk to an adult. My friends never come over any more, and when they do they laugh and say, "I don't see how you stand it!" Then they all drive off to lunch somewhere.

A knock at the back door startled and pleased me. I looked like an advertisement for someone who needed a good iron tonic, but I didn't care.

I opened the door. "Hi," Hilda greeted me, pretending not to notice how I looked. "I haven't seen you in so long; thought I'd check on you." She wore a pantsuit that looked new, and her hair was cut in the latest fashion.

I didn't return her smile. "You don't fool me. You're here because Jerry called you." That gave me unexpected satisfaction. I must have scared him more than he let me know. "He asked you to check on me, didn't he?"

"Nooooo," she said still, smiling. We had been friends and neighbors for over five years. Before the twins were born we often talked about how we "heard the same drum." I could run to borrow a cup of sugar from her and end up sitting at her kitchen table talking for two hours. Late in the evening as I went out to move a bicycle from the driveway, she might be watering her flowers, and we would meet in the street to talk for a moment. We would sit on the curb like children under the streetlight and talk until a husband or a child called us in. Hilda and I had the same sense of humor and compassion. I wished we had been children together; maybe that's why we sometimes acted like children. Hilda was special, but she didn't fool me.

"You haven't been over in months. You never come anymore. You came to check on me," I accused.

Her voice was gentle, pleading. "Marion, let me keep the boys today. I'd love to. I'll play games with them, and it'll be fun for me. You go out. Do whatever you want to. Please."

Oh, God, I want to go—anywhere. I want to.

"No thanks, I'm fine, really—don't need any help."

"Please, Marion."

"I said no!"

I had always been unable to accept help from anyone. I didn't even like to get gifts. I wanted no one to do me a favor.

Hilda had a cup of coffee with me, and somehow the day didn't seem so scary. But during the time we talked, she kept playing with Jon and Jeremy. She seemed really to enjoy them. That made me uncomfortable. Why couldn't I be like that?

I had been invited to a Sunday School meeting later in the week. I declined, of course. I didn't have the energy to go anywhere. I had almost stopped going to Sunday School, but the class kept in touch with me.

Many Sundays Jerry offered to stay home with the boys and let me take the girls. "I'll stay today, Mannie. You go. You need to get out." It was more than a noble offer he knew I'd refuse. His eyes told me he meant it. But I thought he couldn't clean up the house and have lunch ready as I could. Besides, it was such an effort to get ready to go.

So I usually refused, and he took the girls while I stayed home with the twins and cooked a well-balanced Sunday dinner. It never occurred to me we could eat a sandwich. Sometimes we all went, but the thoughts of the way I'd left the house and what we'd have for dinner tortured me.

The night of the class meeting as I loaded the dishwasher, dreading our usual nightly routine, I gently put a dirty plate down and folded the dish towel. The kitchen was still a mess.

I didn't understand my thoughts. *I must go to that meeting tonight. But it's twenty until seven, and Sandy said she would pick me up at ten after seven. I'll never make it.*

But I must go to that meeting. My thoughts continued to argue. *I don't want to go. I want to go to bed. I have to go!*

"Jerry, okay with you if I go to a Sunday School meeting tonight?"

13

"Sure, great. I'll get the children to bed." He sounded pleased.

"Maybe I'll find something there. I have to find something somewhere." I didn't understand that statement, or why I said it. I turned the light off, leaving the kitchen messy for the first time in my life.

In our bedroom I looked into the mirror and hated what I saw. A sad, tired woman looked back at me. I tried to smile. I couldn't.

I dialed Sandy's number. "Can you still pick me up?" She didn't try to hide the surprise in her voice, but assured me that she could.

Dressed, I looked again in the mirror and tried once again to smile. I couldn't. And I didn't want to go. I didn't understand what was happening. *So what? I'm confused a lot lately.*

In the car Sandy and the others talked and laughed, and I felt apart from them. I wanted to run back into the house and forget the whole thing. But I couldn't. Neither could I talk to them. I sat erect and stared straight ahead, listening to the sound of their voices and laughter. It was beautiful, like a waterfall in the desert.

My Sunday School teacher, Bobby Leverett, greeted me. She hugged me. "Oh, I'm so glad *you* came. We hoped you would." I didn't return her enthusiasm. I just stood there looking at her radiant, glowing smile.

"I don't know why I'm here. I didn't want to come. I had to. I'm too tired to be at a class meeting." She put her arm around me briefly again and said in a confident, soft voice, "The Holy Spirit brought you."

Then she walked off to greet someone else. I thought in amazement, Why, she said that like you say, "I'm going to get a loaf of bread." Could it be—could it really be the Holy Spirit who had come into my dirty kitchen in the midst of scraps and crumbs to urge tired, frightened, desperate me to this meeting? Could that possibly be? Does God see me after all?

3

What Makes Her Glow?

Bobby introduced a radiant, smartly dressed young mother, Tricia Jones. I didn't really listen to what Bobby said about her—I watched the speaker. Even before she spoke, she seemed to . . . glow.

Tricia smiled continually, and it seemed natural. I watched her more than I listened to what she said. But she kept talking about a friend—a wonderful, new friend. I thought perhaps she would have her friend come out from another room and speak to us. I certainly would like to meet this friend.

Suddenly I realized she was talking about Jesus Christ. I'd never heard anyone talk about Jesus like that. I wondered if it was all right. She called him "the person, Jesus Christ."

Well, she probably had one well-behaved child and a full-time maid and relatives who fought over who's going to keep the child, I thought.

"I have four children," Tricia explained. "I'm an only child, and all of a sudden here I was at home with four children who continually tracked mud over my carpet. I wanted everything in the house just so, you know?"

Oh, yes, yes, I know!

She continued, "One day I realized I was living from one event to another, only I had this terrible emptiness that kept growing in me. A friend introduced me to Jesus Christ, and nothing has been the same since. I'm a new mother, wife—a new person."

She really had my interest. I listened intently, sitting between friends who later told me they spent much of the evening praying for me.

I wondered if Jesus would help me.

Instantly a thought zoomed in. It never occurred to me that Satan would bother with me. If anyone had told me the thought was from him, I would have laughed—and I didn't laugh easily in those days.

You've been a church member since you were nine. You've worked in Sunday School, and you even used to go Wednesday and Sunday nights. You're a deacon's wife. This is for people who don't go to church. You're getting so desperate, you'll believe anything. You're getting emotional and foolish, too.

My heart pounded as Tricia continued, "Maybe you're a church member. I was a church member, too. But do you know Jesus Christ personally?" She kept glowing and smiling.

I'm not sure, I confessed to myself. I feel so alone and scared and tired—so tired.

Tricia got my attention again with a simple story that was the minute beginning of a new life for me.

"You know, Dick used to leave his underwear in a little pile on the floor every night. I have four children to pick up after, and still he left this neat little pile on the floor each night. I did everything I knew to get him to pick them up or drop them in the hamper. I ignored them for a week, cried, fussed, and pouted." She paused, "But when Christ came into my life he began to give me a different kind of love for my husband. It was not 'I love you when or if,' but an unconditional love. As God began to work in my life, he began causing me to accept Dick just as he was, and I began to gladly pick up his underwear."

Then she laughed on top of glowing, "But the funny thing is, he doesn't throw his underwear down anymore."

It's real. She's telling the truth. All of me agreed. I need what she has. Tricia said she would pray a prayer, and if we wanted Jesus Christ to enter and take control of our lives we could invite him silently.

I bowed my head and with my heart still pounding I prayed: "I need you, Lord Jesus. I thought you were in my heart—maybe you are. But I don't remember ever giving you control. And I don't know exactly how to do it. I just know I need you and I want to know you as a person. Please change me. I need changing."

We had refreshments. Everyone talked. People came to me and asked about the twins. I smiled and told them everything was just fine. Some women went to talk to Tricia. I wanted to, but I stayed in my chair. I didn't want to cry in front of her and all these people.

16

I didn't want to go home. I wanted to stay and listen to people talk about this man, Jesus.

When I got home the breathtaking silence of the house greeted me. An immaculate kitchen warmly welcomed me. Everyone was asleep. I checked on each child, adjusting the cover or just touching a forehead. Jerry was asleep, too.

I looked at him, wanting to tell him about the evening. But I wasn't sure what had happened. I smiled thinking: *You're tired. You had the whole show by yourself tonight. See—it is hard.*

I lay in bed for over an hour feeling something close to happiness. A heavy, iron door had been rapidly closing, shutting me in a darkened room. Now the door had stopped, not quite shut, and a glimmer of light fell on me. I felt it as surely as one feels sunlight upon emerging from a dark, damp tunnel. Maybe I was going to be able to glow, too.

4

Please Help Me

Like a tiny seed, a thought began to grow. I pushed it down. Trod on it. But it grew back. Even as the thought became larger, I pretended it didn't exist. Its message never changed: You need professional help.

I was willing for Jerry to insist on taking me where I could rest and be free of responsibility. But to go and ask for help *myself*—that was something else. The thought stared me in the face early in the morning and followed me around all day. *If I ignore this ridiculous notion, it'll go away.*

I began attending Sunday School and church services more regularly, even though when we arrived my heart pounded and during church my mind pondered what I'd fix for dinner. Then I wondered if the twins were all right in the nursery or if the workers were having trouble with them. I remembered the unmade beds and the crumbs on the kitchen floor. I imagined myself cleaning the house. Even in my mind I couldn't stand it dirty. And then I accused myself: *You should be at home cooking and cleaning up.* But I was drawn to the Sunday School class where mothers openly shared their problems and asked for prayer. They shared answered prayers, too. I couldn't share, but I liked knowing that others had problems, and the idea that God cared about these *little* problems was exciting.

I began to want to read my Bible and pray. My prayers were becoming less and less carefully worded. I prayed like I was talking to a good friend. Sometimes I was close to being happy. But I was still tired much of the time, and I couldn't give up worrying. I even kept a worry list. One day I was worrying about ten things, and I could only remember nine, so I worried about what I'd forgotten to worry about!

I had a goal now, and I couldn't give it up. I wanted to enjoy what I did every day, and I wanted a little time to see if I still existed or if I'd turned into a robot mother.

The thought of seeking help kept growing like a thriving plant. *There is somewhere you can get help.* Finally, I acknowledged the thought.

Well, suppose there is. We can't afford it.

Right back the answer bounced. *It's free!*

Ha . . . fat chance. Nothing's free.

Keep your ears open.

It seemed impossible that a thought could be so powerful. My own argument about it plagued me constantly, although I mentioned it to no one.

I wasn't going down for the third time like the night I took the garbage out. I was treading water now. But I was getting tired. I needed either something to hold onto or the ability to swim without tiring.

I silently answered this stubborn thought about seeking help: *Okay, okay, if I hear of a place that's free that helps mothers who are having a hard time . . . I'll go. I promise.*

One day a neighbor across the street remarked to several of us: "Did you hear about Jackie? She was having trouble with Tommy.

18

He was telling a lot of lies, and she took him to this new place in town that helps mothers with problems—any size problem. And it's free!"

Hilda commented that she thought that was very brave of Jackie to admit she had a problem. They began asking questions. I fled home.

The next week I was attending a Girl Scout function with Julie. I had hoped the boys would behave, but their two-year-old antics forced me to take them outside. There another woman with her child began telling me of a friend of hers. Her friend had such a behavior problem with her little girl that she took her to a new program, an evaluation center. They helped mothers define their problems and eliminate or cope with them.

Ask her where it is, part of me urged. "Maybe that's what I need," I laughed loudly.

"You having problems?"

"Sort of. Something is making my twins too hard to handle. I can't keep up with them. They are too active. I'm not enjoying them." I couldn't tell this stranger that I didn't like myself, either.

"Sure wouldn't hurt to try this place. Here, I'll write down the number for you." She thrust a piece of paper in my hand. For a week I looked at the number periodically. I knew it and the lady's name that I should ask for by heart. *I'll call tomorrow if things aren't better. They're getting better. I don't really need help. I don't want to need help. I can't ask for help.*

Then it started raining. Being shut up with the children, I felt the fog of depression lurking around me. It was closing in on me again. I prayed for the sun, but the rain continued. Panic mounted.

Again and again I went to the phone. I even lifted it off the hook, but I couldn't dial, and I couldn't walk away from the phone.

In the kitchen the boys were screaming and fighting. One of them had poured a box of grits on the floor, and the other one wanted to put the grits back into the box. They fell over one another as they struggled.

My anger frightened me and boiled over into tears. I hadn't cried in a long time. With perspiring hands I dialed the number. A pleasant voice answered: "Rutland Center. May I help you?"

"Laura Levine, please."

"Just a moment. I'll connect you."

"Hello. This is Mrs. Levine."

"Hi, I'm sorry to bother you about something so . . ."

"Could you hold a moment, please?"

It took my remaining strength not to hang up right then.

She was back: "I'm sorry. Please go ahead."

"Well, my problem isn't very big. It's so small I hate to bother you. I keep hearing about your facility—and I do have a problem. Hyperactive twins." I couldn't just say, "I can't cope any more."

"Could you come in next Thursday at 1:30, Mrs. West?"

"Yes, yes. I'll be there. Thank you."

How will I wait? Please hurry, time.

Finally Thursday came. I had arranged for a sitter, and I explained to Jerry: "You see, I keep thinking there's a place that will help me—and it's free. I've been thinking about it for a long time." I imagined what I didn't yet know for certain. "There will be a staff of fifteen people, or so. I think they may watch me with the boys through a two-way mirror—and tell me what's wrong."

Jerry didn't want me to go. I could feel his resistance, but he said: "Go, if you have to. There's nothing wrong with the boys, but I don't care if you go."

As I drove to my appointment, I clenched the steering wheel so hard my knuckles turned white. I licked my dry lips often. Arriving twenty minutes early I pretended to read a *Parent's* magazine. The office was in an old home with creaky doors, high ceilings, and children's drawings taped on the walls. Over my magazine I scrutinized everyone and listened to their conversations.

"Mrs. West, Mrs. Levine can see you now." Mrs. Levine's warm smile was just what I needed. It seemed like sunshine, even though I sat stiffly holding my back erect and trying very hard to look at ease.

"I'm afraid something's wrong with my twins, and I know there's something wrong with me."

In the first five minutes of my interview, Mrs. Levine strongly recommended a psychiatrist for me. "Right away," she added, trying to mask her concern.

I babbled: "No, I believe I'm supposed to get help from a mother of four children, and the help will be free. I know I can't talk to a man. You can help me. How many children do you have?"

I was dumbfounded at my definite stand. Decisions had become almost impossible for me. Where to park—what to buy at the grocery store—whether to stroll the boys or sit in the yard with them—whether to talk to Jerry or keep my troubles to myself . . .

"I have four children, but Mrs. West, you need a psychiatrist—today. I can recommend one. You'll like him."

Please, God, let her help me.

"Please help me, Mrs. Levine."

She hesitated and then smiled that wonderful, warm smile again: "All right. Let's get started." She questioned me for over an hour, writing on the side of her questionnaire and in the margins.

Finally, I glanced at the clock. "I've been here almost two hours. I was only supposed to have an hour appointment. I'm sorry. I've taken too much of your time."

"It's all right. Keep talking. How long since you've talked about things that are bothering you?"

I could have talked all day. It was like throwing away old clothes from the attic that should have been discarded years ago. "I don't know. I can't seem to stop. I'm sorry."

"Talk," she encouraged, "Don't be sorry." Before I left, she said, "Let me assure you of one thing. From what you've told me, there is absolutely nothing wrong with your twins." And in a softer voice, "It's you, Mrs. West . . . you're working too hard at motherhood. You'll never make it this way."

Nothing wrong with your twins! What a beautiful statement. It was me then—and *I* could change. I wanted to change. This mother with four children and the warm understanding smile was going to help me change.

Thank you, God, that I found her.

5

The World's Still Here

Our whole family entered the Rutland Center program. The center's policy was to involve fathers in their program for a few weeks. Jerry agreed, with some reservation. I was grateful to him. He promised he'd meet me there at the appointed time. He arrived just a few minutes late. I was already in Mrs. Levine's office. He came in smiling at me and greeted Mrs. Levine enthusiastically. He even thought of something amusing to say, and we all laughed. I felt good. I was so glad he was smiling with his eyes. But when we began to talk I clammed up—looking only at Mrs. Levine. I was afraid to look at Jerry for a reason I didn't understand.

I felt a wall separated us.

Finally we left, and as we walked to the car a low branch hung in our path over the sidewalk. It was right in our faces. I had to pass it everytime I left the Center. I bent over and scrambled underneath it. It had been raining, and I got my face wet. Jerry let go of my hand and simply stepped out on the curb and went around. The simplicity of his reaction to the obstacle in our path startled me and gave me an unexpected look at myself and my approach to life. As we met on the other side, we rejoined hands laughing. We were thinking the same thoughts, and it brought us closer together. We both looked back toward Mrs. Levine's window, and she was watching us. She laughed, too. Without uttering a word, they both communicated to me, "See, Marion, you don't have to do everything the hard way."

On our second visit he reached out and touched my hand and said, "Mannie . . ." and I think I spent the rest of the time looking gratefully at him.

For almost a year I had had a recurring dream. I dreaded it. The dream was always the same. The children and I were in a deep, fast-moving river. We were being rushed toward a waterfall. I tried to hold onto the children and save myself, too. But it was useless—we were all going to be swept over the waterfall.

Then I saw Jerry standing alone on a lush green bank, admiring new clothes he'd just bought. He was looking at his reflection in the water. *Call to him,* a part of me urged. But most of me insisted, *Never mind. He's too busy. Besides he won't get his clothes all wet just to help you. Prepare to go over the waterfall.* Then I would wake up crying. I didn't tell Jerry about the dream until I dreamed the ending the night after he touched my hand in Mrs. Levine's office.

As I started approaching the waterfall, the dream continued in a new way. I called out loudly: "Jerry, help me. Help us!"

He threw off his new coat and jumped into the water and pulled all of us out. I kept saying: "You got your new clothes all wet for us. You saved us. You do care. You really do."

He was laughing gratefully and holding me: "Of course, I care. I didn't see you. Why didn't you call me sooner?"

There was another dream. In it I was lost. I could see a certain building that I needed to reach. It was tall and clean and well-lighted. But I kept taking a wrong turn into the slums. I was terribly frightened. Night approached and everybody knew where to go, except me. Fear consumed me. I tried so many streets. I cut through alleys and fields and climbed over fences. I ran till I nearly dropped. I followed other people only to become lost again. The building remained in sight, but I never could find the way to it.

One night this dream changed, too. I walked up to someone and said: "I'm lost. Can you help me?"

"Certainly," the friendly stranger replied. "Follow me." This stranger was taking me to the beautiful building, but I wanted to ask others to help me to see if they would. Everyone I asked wanted to help me.

The stranger took me to the front door of the building, and it was even more beautiful than I had imagined. I felt safe here. Just before I entered the door I promised myself: *I'll never forget how horrible it is to be lost. Others are still lost in those dark alleys. I'll help anyone find this wonderful, well-lighted building. I hope I can show someone the way.*

23

At the Rutland Center, exactly in accordance with my premonition, I became the first mother to be observed through a two-way mirror with my children. Feeling awkward at first, I followed a prescribed playtime with Jon and Jeremy. I intended to accept all the help available.

"You talk too much to them. Listen, instead," Mrs. Levine suggested.

Even Julie and Jennifer asked to be included in the program. Mrs. Levine graciously talked with each girl, much to their delight.

Now came something more difficult. Mrs. Levine said sternly one day, "You must put the twins in nursery school and do something you really like doing." She seemed to sense my resistance. But she insisted, "I can't help you anymore if you won't put them in a nursery."

As I began thinking about a nursery school, words like "desert" and "cop-out" banged around in my mind. The boys weren't yet two and a half!

You'll ruin their future, putting them in school so young. It's cruel. Don't leave them. Remember how it was when your mother had to go to work when your daddy died. You were just a few months younger than they are. You don't have to leave your children. Stay home with them. Remember how you wanted your mother to stay with you? Remember that pain?

Oh, yes! I remember. I won't leave them. But Mrs. Levine said I must. I trust Mrs. Levine, don't I? Of course I do . . . but suppose she's wrong this one time?

I have to trust she's right.

I made inquiries. Two nursery schools wouldn't consider them because Jeremy could climb over a chain-link fence. I felt relief. I wouldn't have to send them after all. But a part of me insisted, *Let me be free for a little while. I have to.*

Then a third school accepted the twins. With a lump in my throat I took them the first time. "You understand Jeremy can climb over your fence and will be in the street in a second. He climbs like a monkey." I was still holding firmly onto their hands.

Gently, Mrs. Crowley, a grandmotherly lady, eased them away

24

from me. "They will be fine. I promise. We'll see you at one."

I stood there unable to move or speak.

"Good-bye, Mrs. West."

"Do you have my number and the number of my friend? Would you like for me to stay for a while and . . ."

"We'll see you later. Say good-bye, boys." Mrs. Crowley walked off with Jon and Jeremy. For a moment I thought I would run and grab them and drive off. I wanted to take them home and build castles with them in the sandpile, make peanut butter and jelly sandwiches to eat under the weeping willow tree, read books, and watch butterflies.

But you can't do that eighteen hours a day. You've tried as hard as anyone could try. This is a little bit of freedom. Take it.

I walked out, blinking tears away. I turned the car around in the driveway and waited for a few moments. If Jeremy broke loose I'd catch him.

Finally I drove off. *Watch over them, God. I love them so much. They're the youngest little people there. They're still in diapers. Let everybody be nice to them.*

It wasn't a particularly beautiful day, but as I drove down a familiar street and looked up at the sky for a moment, suddenly it was the most beautiful day in the world. I felt, tiptoeing around the edges of my heart, happiness. Then it came crashing in on me like giant waves on a beach.

I said aloud, "The world's still here—and I'm part of it again."

6

Here's Your Change

Jerry and I also consented to enter the twins in a special program at Rutland Center for children with behavior problems.

I was realizing now, even though Mrs. Levine had not spelled it out for me, that deep down I had wanted Jon to match Jeremy.

And they were so different. In the recovery room they had shown me Jeremy first—then Jon. My comment had been, "But they don't match!"

I tried to laugh off that remark, but somehow it never became funny, and my attitude affected Jon's personality somewhat. He had become loud and demanding and insisted that he wanted to be like Jeremy—to the point of copying him. I didn't like that either.

And Jon felt all this.

I was trying to undo my mistake, and the Center was helping tremendously. Every Tuesday I still met with Mrs. Levine, and we continued to work out my part of the problem.

Another thing I had to admit to myself was that I totally rejected help of any kind. I recalled something that had happened when Jennifer had her tonsils removed. She was barely four when the doctor said her tonsils must come out. She was weakened from throat and bladder infections. I didn't know then that God could give me peace during my child's surgery. I spent sleepless nights prior to the operation trying to pray.

One night as I prayed I finally said: "God, I *have* to have an answer from you. Some kind of communication. I have to know you hear me. Tell me Jennifer will not die." This was an unusual prayer for me. In those days my bedtime prayer was something like, "Bless the world and everybody everywhere and help the starving people. Help me in everything and take care of the children. Amen." I wanted for him to answer. It was nearly two in the morning. My pillow was wet from crying. Words slipped into my mind. They didn't seem to be my words.

"She's going to be all right. She's going to be all right, Marion . . . *you* are too!"

He answered me. God answered me! I sat up in bed. *He knows my name. And God has a sense of humor. And Jennifer is going to be fine.*

I was asleep before my head hit the pillow. But by morning Satan was doing a good job of convincing me it was all my imagination. The fear came back. I didn't know how to deal with it.

Jennifer, of course, came through the surgery fine. I stayed with her all night. I went home the day after her surgery to wash her favorite blanket on which she had thrown up.

I knew I must ask my next door neighbor, Anne Litaker, for the use of her dryer. We didn't have one. But Anne had already insisted on keeping Julie while Jennifer was in the hospital. Over my protests she had taken Julie's hand and led her home with her.

How could I let someone keep my child? The thought made me uncomfortable. But then I decided what I'd do. As Anne took the blanket out of the dryer, I reached into my pocket and pulled out an envelope with her name on it.

"What's this?" she looked surprised.

I smiled securely. "Something for you." I drove back to the hospital with the warm blanket on my lap and thinking about Anne's eyes. They held hurt when I gave her the envelope. But she would find something she wanted with the ten dollars.

The next day Jennifer was to come home. Again, Anne had insisted on drying a load of her things for me. As I gathered them up to leave Anne said, "Marion, here's your change."

"My what?"

"Your change." Her eyes twinkled. The twinkles turned to sparkles as her eyes filled with tears. I put the clothes basket down and took the envelope she gave me. It was heavy. I opened it. Quarters, nickels, dimes, and half dollars.

"What . . ."

"It's your change for keeping Julie. Ten dollars worth of change. I love you. Let me do things for you." She hugged me, wiped her eyes, and put the envelope on my dried clothes, silencing any protests I might have made by opening the door for me. As I started home, Anne called out, "Tell Jen I'll be over soon."

I tried desperately to convince myself Anne was wrong and stubborn to give me all my money back . . . but I never could. I wanted to be able to accept help and gifts. I admired people who could. Why couldn't I? I needed to change. I had been wrong.

It was nearly two years later, again in a hospital, that I accepted one of the dearest gifts anyone ever offered me. I needed it desperately. And I accepted it gratefully.

7

Rosemary's Gift

So this is what it's like to watch your child die. My mouth was so dry I couldn't swallow. This is fear—raw fear consuming me. I can't believe this is happening, and yet I'm watching it. It has to be real. *Jeremy is dying. One of my nine-month-old twins is dying. Then I will have just one little boy. I must prepare to give him up.*

I tried to prepare, but I continued to pray silently the shortest prayer of my life: *Please, God.*

And in the back of my mind, I reasoned, if he'd been admitted to the hospital sooner—if the medication had been changed sooner—if the doctors hadn't insisted it was the flu like everyone else had—if I'd called the doctor back last night, even if it was late, like I wanted to . . . if, if, if . . .

Jeremy had stopped screaming now. He had cried almost all night. For three days he had been seriously ill with a fever that often climbed to 105°. As we waited to see the doctor this morning, he had screamed—a loud piercing, unusual scream. I had sat holding him and crying silently, not caring that people stared. Jerry had tried to reassure me, but I saw open fear in his eyes.

Jeremy's head was swollen grotesquely. A bluish-purple abscess jutted from his right cheek. The inside of his throat was swollen almost closed so that he fought for breath. The doctors, of course, sent us to the hospital with "stat" orders. Crying, I ran past admissions, and up the stairs with him, taking him to a nurse I saw that I knew.

She couldn't hide her concern. His room was not available yet. A tiny examining room quickly filled with people working over him. Lab technicians tried to get blood and urine samples. Someone mentioned the possibility of a tracheotomy. Now Jeremy wasn't moving or crying. He stared at the ceiling.

Our pastor, Jim Griffith, came. He, Jerry, and I watched silently.

28

I became acutely aware of the looks the nurses exchanged. They tried to smile at me. Then everyone left momentarily. It was a nightmare in slow motion. Couldn't they move faster? Too much precious time had been wasted. I heard someone say his temperature was near 107°.

Jeremy's eyes seemed to change—they glazed over and rolled back in his head. I had been taking his pulse. It stopped. "Jeremy!" I screamed.

"He's all right. He's all right," Jerry said in a strange voice. Our pastor ran to get help. Seconds later a nurse came running into the room and grabbed Jeremy as if he were a rag doll. She ran with him to the end of the hall where another nurse had cold water running from the tap. Together they put him under it.

The nurse who had grabbed Jeremy usually worked in the intensive care unit. She was filling in on pediatrics today. She was used to life and death situations and acting quickly. *I'll never forget you. Even if he's dead. I see how hard you are trying. Thank you.*

Was it too late to pray for his life? No, they were running with him to his room. I felt like I was fainting, but decided I couldn't—not now. I ran after them.

This wonderful nurse began packing Jeremy in ice. *No, I can still pray. She's still working with him. God bless her.* "Get ice on his head," she commanded. *Oh, finally I could do something for him.* I packed ice furiously on the small hot head. Others continued to cover his body in ice.

And then—the most beautiful sound in the world. He opened his eyes and screamed! Screamed loud and long.

I laughed. I couldn't stop laughing. Other people in the room were laughing. Our neighbors, Hilda and Earl, arrived just then. We were all laughing, and Jeremy was screaming strong, healthy screams of life. Even as I laughed, I prayed: "Thank you. Oh, thank you, God."

In a short while Jeremy stood up in the little bed and uttered his entire vocabulary. Never in his nine months of life had I enjoyed the sound of his voice so dearly, "Mama, daddy, dog. Whe' bro?" It was his first separation from Jon.

I refused to leave him, staying by his side day and night. Even when I became exhausted and the nurses asked me to go home, I refused. I stood guard over him like a mother tiger.

As I guarded him, I realized bitterness was eating up the gratitude. I wanted to get rid of it, but I didn't know how. The thoughts wouldn't go away. My baby had almost died, and it should never have happened. I knew it wasn't an ordinary illness on that first day when he became sick. I knew it wasn't the flu. But the doctors had tagged me a hysterical mother. They should have believed me and watched him more closely.

And why hadn't they changed his medication after no improvement in three days? Why had Jeremy been forced to come so close to death as I watched? Why did Jerry and I have to live through that nightmare?

When I slept, I dreamed the whole scene over and awakened in terror. And I couldn't bring myself to look in the little examining room where his pulse had stopped. My resentment fastened on a hatred of that room. It was as if I wanted that room torn out of the hospital.

"Forget it, Mannie. It's over. Jeremy's all right," Jerry tried to help me. I knew he had no bitterness about what happened. It was obvious in his face. His joy was apparent every time he walked into Jeremy's room to pick him up. He would silently hold him close for a moment before playing with him in his usual clowning way that Jeremy loved. All Jerry felt was gratitude. I felt him watching me for signs that I wasn't reliving the past.

But I was. I became silent, staring straight ahead and thinking that I'd never forgive the doctors. I was so withdrawn at one point that Jerry had our family doctor come by to talk with me. After that I made an effort to pretend things were better. But I didn't fool Jerry. "We have so much to be thankful for, Mannie," he would tell me. I heard his voice and I knew he was right, but this resentment was stronger than any I'd ever been caught in. "Dear God, I hate this bitterness. All I should feel is gratitude. Forgive my bitterness—take it away, somehow."

Jeremy fit into the smallest wheelchair I'd ever seen, and he loved to be strolled in the halls. It was two days before Christmas. A gingerbread tree stood by the elevator. We always stopped to look at it. I turned my head away from the little examining room each time we passed it. I wanted to look at it and stop being afraid. But bitterness welled up in my heart and I reminded myself, "It should never have happened."

Most of the children had gone home for Christmas. Only a few remained. I peeked into the room next to ours late in the afternoon. A small black girl looked out at us—then she looked away.

"Hi," I smiled at her.

She wouldn't look at me. I read her name on the door. "Rosemary?" She looked at me. "If you ever want to come out and stroll with us, we'd love to have you." I saw a small wheelchair in the corner of her room. The next morning as I came out of Jeremy's room, Rosemary sat there by our door in her wheelchair waiting for us.

"Hey, Rosemary." She didn't answer but began rolling her chair to keep up with us. I talked to her but didn't know if she heard me or even if she could speak. She seemed almost in a trance. Soon a nurse came and put her back in bed.

"How is she?" I asked the nurse when we were alone. She shook her head and looked away. "Will she be all right?" I persisted.

"She's retarded and a cripple. Has severe kidney problems and about four other major illnesses. She's in and out of here all the time."

"What are her . . . chances?"

The nurse shook her head and looked away again, leaving hurriedly. I followed her. "Do her parents come often?"

"Can't come too much. They have other children, and they both work."

"But tomorrow is Christmas."

The nurse ran to answer the phone.

Throughout the day I would go outside my door and find Rosemary waiting. I learned to recognize the squeak of her chair. Christmas Eve I went out and found her. "Want to come watch me bathe Jeremy?"

She smiled faintly and nodded her head. I was overjoyed at her

31

response. I helped her get her small wheelchair into the little bathroom. I was holding Jeremy on my hip as I filled the tub. He squirmed, anxious to get into the water. It was difficult to hold him.

"Let me hold Jeremy for you," Rosemary offered. Even before I looked up, I knew I must not hesitate. "Thank you, Rosemary. Hold him tight. He's strong." She reached her arms up for Jeremy, and he reached for her. Instantly she encircled him with both arms, holding him closely and securely. Jeremy relaxed and snuggled close to her, playing with one of her pigtails.

"I'll take him now, Rosemary. Thank you." She smiled proudly, "You're welcome."

After Jeremy and Rosemary were asleep, I asked one of the nurses if I could have Jerry bring Rosemary some presents for Christmas. She seemed pleased.

Jerry said he could get some toys as well as fruit and candy. Suddenly I thought of something. "See if the girls mind if you bring the talking doll. She's just like new."

It was a strange Christmas Eve. I was without my family. I didn't feel like Christmas, and the hospital didn't smell like Christmas. It was quiet and almost empty. I looked out Jeremy's window at the lights below and at the Christmas trees . . . and the starry sky. I slept soundly that night . . . not even waking to check on Jeremy several times like I had been doing.

Jerry arrived early with the gifts. When I gave Rosemary the doll she pulled its string, and the doll asked, "What is the color of my dress? Can you tie your shoes?" Rosemary's face glowed in happiness. She hugged the doll to her.

Our doctor came by and said Jeremy could go home. Jeremy had been the victim of a very rare infection. Now he was all right.

Jerry went to the hospital office to see about the bill, and I began packing Jeremy's things. I went to tell Rosemary good-bye. I didn't know what to say. I just stood there holding Jeremy on my hip.

"You going home, Jeremy boy! You be good for your mama, you hear?" Rosemary said. "You gon' be fine."

I sat on the edge of her bed and hugged her, and Jeremy grabbed one of her pigtails and wouldn't let go. As I gently pulled him away he brought the doll with him. I attempted to take it away from him. Rosemary said, "Let him have it."

"No, Rosemary. She's yours."

"But I want to give Jeremy something for Christmas."

"Oh, you've given Jeremy so much . . . and me, too. I couldn't have made it without you, Rosemary. I'm going to tell Jeremy about you when he gets bigger. I'd even like to write a story about you someday."

"Me . . . a story about me?"

I nodded my head.

"And you gon' tell Jeremy boy about me, you won't forget?"

"I won't forget."

I handed the doll back, pretending humor, "Boys aren't supposed to play with dolls."

"That's right. I'll keep her then. I named her Katherine. Do you like that name?"

"I love it."

I had to go but couldn't seem to leave. "Thank you for . . . helping me, Rosemary."

"You're welcome," she smiled. And I just stood there looking at a little girl with no future as she held a doll and smiled at me.

My eyes brimmed as I hurried from her room and went down the hall. I didn't look at the Christmas tree. I stopped and looked directly into the examining room. I stared long and hard. Bitterness and fear vanished completely and my heart pounded with gratitude.

As I pushed the button for the elevator the mechanical question floated down the empty hall, "Can you tie your shoes? What is the color of my dress?"

8

Don't Cry, Mama

I continued daily to be grateful that Jeremy was alive. When he ate an orange or ran from me laughing or chased a butterfly, I thought, *You almost missed this.*

It was the March when the twins were a year old that Julie talked to Jerry and me about Jesus and salvation. Our pastor talked with her. She wasn't yet nine. But I remembered once, before she was three, I had been discouraged about something. We were sitting out in the yard together. I pondered my problem thoughtfully, looking down at the ground. Suddenly her hand touched my face gently, "Look your face up, Mama, and see God."

Early one morning just after she was three I had found her out in her gown looking at our morning glories. "What are you doing?" I demanded. "Did you know God made the morning smell the best?" she answered.

And it had been Julie, barely eight years old, who became concerned about the fact that I smoked. Without my knowing it, she prayed daily that cigarettes would make me sick and that I would stop smoking. One day she grinned a victorious smile as she watched me crush one out and go to lie down, complaining of a sick feeling. As soon as I saw her smile, I knew what she had been doing. And I knew she disapproved of anyone smoking.

"Julie, you've been praying, haven't you?"

"Yes, Mama, and it's working."

That was the last cigarette I ever smoked, or wanted to smoke. Even to see them in the grocery store made me feel ill.

I wasn't surprised when she began talking to her daddy and me about going forward Sunday morning during the hymn of invitation. "I believe it'll be this Sunday, Mama. Please don't cry. I know you'll cry, and I'm going to pray you don't."

"You better pray for your grandmother, too. She'll be with us on Sunday."

"Okay," she smiled.

For the remainder of the week I prayed not to cry . . . and that my mother wouldn't either. And as I prayed, I cried. I shed my tears in advance.

I had never heard the song before that we sang at the close of the Sunday service. I listened carefully to the words.

"Out of my bondage, sorrow, and night, Jesus, I come, Jesus, I come."

Julie stepped out and went forward. I stopped singing and thanked God. Julie was making it known that she trusted Jesus Christ as her Savior. As the pastor introduced Julie, she seemed to glow. I'd never seen her so beautiful or so sure of what she was doing. I looked over, and my mother wasn't crying. But I heard something. Then I looked at Jerry. No one had thought to pray for him. I had only seen him cry one time before and somehow it seemed right that he should now.

I realized now that I had a judgmental attitude towards Jerry. I wanted him to experience things the same way I did, and I thought that my displays of emotion moved me up higher than he on the "spiritual ladder." But more than surprise and satisfaction, I felt closeness to him. He went down to stand by Julie, and I joined them. Then it seemed all right that the three of us wept together.

Two weeks later they sang that song again one evening, and I went forward for rededication. I wanted to confirm that I belonged to Christ, and I asked God to make me a better wife and mother. But I still felt there was something more I could do. I didn't know what.

I began thinking a lot about the cross. The first time we visited Beech Haven Baptist Church, they were meeting in a small, simple building. As we entered it, I looked up at a little handmade wooden cross over the door. We had always belonged to a large ornate church where the cross was not so much in evidence . . . not a little wooden one just a few feet above my head, anyway.

I thought people weren't supposed to think about the cross. Later, I noticed some people talked about it. The same people who talked about Jesus so openly.

35

I thought of Jesus (when I thought of him at all) as the man in the picture on the cardboard fan I saw as a child. His appearance rather feminine, he wore a purple robe and his face was sad as he knelt by a large rock. Was this the Jesus everyone seemed to be talking about?

I couldn't figure out the cross. *What's it got to do with me? It's ugly. How could it . . . save . . . (that was hard to say) anyone? I didn't have anything to do with Jesus dying on the cross. He did it for the world . . . not for me. Please, not for me. Maybe it didn't hurt, anyway. He was God, wasn't he?*

Then I would remember what Tricia had said. I thought she looked right at me. "If you had been the only person in the world, Jesus would have gladly died for you. But you must accept personally his loving sacrifice for you."

How can I accept such a gift? It's not real to me. I can't even say his name without effort? Then I wondered, *Does this same Jesus watch over me?*

Once I had looked at a map of the United States Julie was using in a school assignment. I thought, there are so many places I could be. And here I am. I touched the upper middle of Georgia. I've hardly moved half an inch in my life. Maybe I'm supposed to be way over here . . . I slid my hand toward California . . . or up here . . . I touched New England. I'm not sure where I belong. Only one life . . . and I'm not sure I'm living it like I'm supposed to. I keep hearing about a "plan for your life." How can I know the plan for sure?

I noticed a few people who seemed incredibly happy, regardless of their circumstances. I wanted to be like that. But Satan, it must have been he, told me: "No, those people were born to be happy. You were not. You can't have that quality."

But what if I can have it? What if that peace is meant for me?

When Julie accepted Christ I examined my own life more closely. But my questions remained unanswered.

The next year Jennifer went forward, accepting Jesus also; and deep inside me I had to admit that my "God-shaped vacuum" wasn't yet full.

9

Help's on the Way

I guess it was Anne who first introduced me to the idea of praying about small things. It was before the twins were born. I argued fiercely with her that you couldn't bother God with little things. She wouldn't agree . . . nor would she argue. She just went on praying for a Christian maid. It could be chance that she found one, I insisted. Her Sunday School class grew in number and in spirit, and I knew that she prayed for the members individually.

I watched her as she accepted the news that her oldest son must face bone surgery. There was a good possibility it might be malignant. Her faith never wavered . . . and Wayne didn't have cancer.

One day she told me she was going to pray that Frank and her boys would build her a rose trellis for her climbing rose. It was growing out across their lawn. She said it with the same sincerity that she had asked me to pray for Wayne when he faced skin grafts. The next week I watched from my window as Frank and the three boys built the rose trellis. *It couldn't be an answered prayer, could it?*

Anne seemed nearly as thrilled as I was to learn I was pregnant. Jerry and I had wanted another baby for over a year.

I'll never forget the day my obstetrician sent me to be X-rayed. I was almost seven months pregnant but looked past due. My doctors had avoided my constant question, "Do you think it's twins?" At last I'd know for sure.

Jennifer, not quite five, had said when we told her a baby was on the way, "It'll be twins. One for Julie and one for me." We laughed at her childlike reasoning. She always referred to the baby as "they." By the time I was six months pregnant, we stopped laughing. "You'll see," she insisted, "it's twins."

The doctor who took the X-rays held up his index and middle finger and grinned at me. I thought he was making a "V" for victory sign. He had to tell me. "Twins, Mrs. West! It's twins. They look nice and large."

Instantly my mouth was as dry as cotton, and I felt wonderfully happy. *Me, twins!* Almost in shock while I drove home, I repeated aloud, "I'm having twins." I still couldn't believe it. I ran two red lights.

I rang Anne's doorbell and when she saw the silly expression on my face, she screamed, "It's twins!" We went from door to door around the neighborhood. When each door was opened, I just stood there grinning, and Anne made the announcement, "It's twins."

I called Jerry and invited him home for lunch. I wanted to see his face when I told him. He probably thought I'd messed up the checkbook again when I asked him to come home. The minute he walked in I said, "We're having twins."

His grin came as if in slow motion. "Are you sure?"

"The doctor said for you to come see the X-ray. He said he knew you'd want to see for yourself—daddies always did." Jerry took pictures of the X-rays and showed them proudly around his office. I was glad he was so happy about the babies.

Before the babies arrived, Anne moved away. She knew we were having trouble finding help for me after the arrival of the twins. As soon as we thought we had a woman lined up to help us, she cancelled out. Anne had told me before she moved, "Pray, Marion. God'll send help." But I just couldn't pray about that.

The day Anne moved I cried all day. I pulled down the shades next to her carport so I couldn't see the moving truck. I wanted to give her something. On my kitchen wall hung a painting which I had done of an old house. There was a feeling of love and friendship in the painting, I thought. Anne had always liked it.

I took it down and wrapped it, huffing and puffing. My stomach was so big I could hardly bend over. I couldn't carry it far so I drove next door. When Anne opened the door I was crying, and Anne's eyes filled. Only Anne could cry and look pretty . . . smiling through tears. My face crumpled like tissue paper. We didn't say anything. I just handed it to her and drove back home.

On March 1, 1968, our twin sons were born. Jerry called our parents and friends at 2:30 A.M. Everytime I saw him, he was grinning.

Our babies were quite obviously fraternal. I had expected girls again and was amazed and delighted to learn we had sons. But I had somehow assumed they would be identical.

The day before I was to leave the hospital, Anne called long distance. "Do you have help yet?"

"No."

"Well, it's on the way. I've been on my knees praying for you and I know God has answered my prayers." *Same ol' Anne.* Fifteen minutes later Jerry walked into my room with a young woman. She smiled shyly.

"I think we have found our help." Jerry seemed terribly pleased. "This is Edna. I put an ad in the paper the day before you came to the hospital, and she just answered it."

"Did Jerry tell you we have two other children and how little we can pay?"

"He told me. I'll do everything I can to help you. I love children. I just hope I can please you and that you'll let me come and try."

I nodded gratefully. I had expected a much older woman. I didn't know how I'd feel about Edna doing things for us. We were nearly the same age. And I couldn't figure out why she wanted the job. She seemed even happier than I was about it.

Well, the main thing, I'll have help when we get home. I won't need her for long. Just a while at first. Anne's faith and prayer had brought Edna to us. I knew that. It didn't just happen.

10

Is She Your Sister?

Edna served my favorite food, a banana and peanut butter sandwich on a small tray. "I won't be in bed long," I assured her. "You won't have to do things for me . . . just the babies."

"I don't mind doing things for you if I can please you."

"I'm not hard to please. But all you have to do is help with the babies."

"Is your sandwich all right?"

"Best I ever had."

Without warning she said, "You're not stuck up at all. When I first saw you in the hospital I thought you'd be real mean and stuck up." I didn't know how to respond, but she didn't seem to notice. "While the boys are asleep I'm going to do some cleaning."

"Please don't do that," I begged.

"I want to. Your house is so pretty. It's just dirty." I had neglected it the last two months before the babies came when I could hardly move, much less clean.

She scrubbed walls and woodwork and cleaned under beds. She picked up continually as she walked through the house, and she waxed the floors. Edna always started supper each afternoon before she left. When she discovered how much we loved biscuits but that I couldn't make them, she left a pan of them in the oven.

One day she dyed my bedroom rug green because she heard me say I wanted a green rug. For Easter, she made Julie and Jennifer and me matching dresses. We wore them to church.

When my friends stopped by those first few weeks to see the babies, Edna served coffee and cake, but I could never get her to stop cleaning long enough to sit with us. She fussed over the babies like they were hers as she brought them out for everyone to see.

As some of my friends were leaving one day, I heard one say, "Who is that wonderful girl staying with Marion?"

"I don't know. Maybe it's her sister. They look alike."

Another friend asked, "Is Edna your sister?"

As we became close friends Edna told me she had three boys. They were in a children's home. They came to visit her a while each summer and at Christmas. Her life, from her teens, was like things I had only read about. I listened, hurting for her, trying not to show shock as she talked.

Edna had worked in a clothing factory making three times what she made working for us. For some reason, she suddenly wanted to be with children and a family and in a home situation. Then she had seen Jerry's ad in the paper. I knew Edna was temporary help. We couldn't afford her much longer, and some days I sensed she was getting restless.

Saturday I went to the mailbox. I opened a letter written in an unfamiliar handwriting. "I'm not coming back, Marion. I'm going back to work in the factory. I just couldn't tell you in person. Kiss the boys for me and don't forget me. Please don't be mad at me. Love, Edna."

The letter wasn't a surprise, but managing everything without Edna was a traumatic experience. I became short with the girls and Jerry. Jerry hardly got in the door before I started complaining, often crying. He must have dreaded coming home, but he always came in smiling. I even began resenting his smile.

Edna and I kept in touch by phone. When she came to visit us one day, she brought her own three sons to visit us.

When we learned her mother had died, Jerry and I went to see her. I thought we'd never find her trailer. When we did, she grabbed me around the neck, sobbing, "You came." I gave her a little book about God's love for each of us in all situations. She told me over and over how much she loved that book.

About three years later we were eating out one Sunday after church. I was busy trying to get the boys settled. They were screaming for food. I felt someone watching me and looked. People often stared as we attempted to get the boys quiet in a restaurant. It was Edna. She smiled. Her hair was soaking wet, still dripping on her dress.

"I just got baptized," she said softly. "I'm so happy!"

"Oh, Edna, that's wonderful. I'm happy for you."

She joined her party at another table, but as we ate I looked over at her and thought, "She *is* my sister now. We are sisters in Christ."

11

Help Someone

Although many of my spiritual questions remained unanswered, my emotional problems began to be resolved. After about six weeks of our sessions, Mrs. Levine insisted I find a hobby. "What do you like?" she asked.

"Hospitals," I replied quickly.

"Hospitals!"

I nodded my head and explained, "I did volunteer work when the girls were small. I love it."

"Do it again," she said firmly. Then she smiled at me, "Please Mrs. West. You must do it."

I sat in the Athens General Hospital waiting room swinging my foot impatiently and thinking: *This is crazy. I have no business volunteering for anything. I'm the one who needs help. Why do I think I can help someone? Why couldn't I help myself? Big deal . . . I'm going to help someone!*

I sat with the other new volunteers waiting for a Pink Lady to come give us instructions. She came rushing to us, apologizing for being late. "Ready, ladies?" she asked. "Let's go see where you'll be working."

Oh, dear Lord, not a tour of the hospital, please. This isn't what I need. I don't want to be in a large group of people. I just want to help one person . . . and I hate guided tours.

Clomp, clomp, we marched to the elevator. The volunteers . . . the nurse's friend and helper . . . the deliverer of flowers and writer of notes . . . the cheerful, smiling volunteer in pink.

As we got off the elevator, the smell of a hospital surrounded us, and I breathed it in deeply. Why do I love this smell? It is comfortable. It makes me feel secure. Why? I thought back to my childhood.

I had been sick often. I came close to dying with scarlet fever when I was three. For years after that I was susceptible to strep throat and pneumonia. There were kidney complications. I was often a patient at the little hospital in Elberton. I was afraid of needles, and always required injections. But I liked the attention the nurses gave me and all the constant activity at the hospital.

Sometimes I just needed the shots but didn't need to be put to bed. A routine developed. I stayed at the hospital "helping out" while my mother worked at the bank. Dr. Walton Johnson was a close friend of ours. Many of the nurses were my mother's friends.

Someone made me a little Red Cross uniform for Christmas. It was of thick white material and had a big red cross sewn on the front. A hat matched. It became my official uniform while I "helped out."

I visited with patients waiting to see the doctor. Little girls asked about my uniform and what I did. Often I sat on a white stool in the lab and inhaled all the unfamiliar smells like a child sniffing good aromas in a kitchen. I soon learned to enjoy the smell of ether and alcohol. I soaked up hospital language, and I watched Dr. Johnson and Dr. D. N. Thompson at work. I especially loved watching their hands. Even when they weren't treating sick people, I looked at their hands in open fascination.

And I adored the big, old medical books that I stretched on tiptoe to reach. I carefully lifted them down to dust them, but soon found myself looking at the amazing pictures in them.

It was well worth taking the shots to get to stay here and "help out." The nurses asked me to do things for them—not just to entertain me—but real errands. When I insisted that I had to see "Doc" to ask him something important, he opened the door to his office and motioned me in, listening carefully to my problem. Then he told me exactly what to do as if I were a nurse.

The Pink Lady interrupted my thoughts: "You. I'll show you how to make a bed."

Dear Lord, what will she say if I cry all over the clean sheets? Did I leave a dirty house and five unmade beds to have seven ladies watch me learn to make a bed properly?

"Good," she praised my efforts. "You'll be making beds in no

43

time."

Not if I can help it. I want to work with people, not beds.

That night I prayed, "Lord, give me one person to help. Just one person. There must be someone. Someone special. Anybody."

I had not been in the program long before a young, almost arrogant girl asked a group of us one day: "Are any of you interested in doing something new and different? It'll be direct patient contact. It won't appeal to most people. It's hard work." Her name was Scout Gunn, Dr. Scout Gunn, and she was in charge of the new recreational therapy program.

I was the only Pink Lady who was interested. I liked Scout's determined attitude. "I need someone to work in the psychiatric department and other areas," she told six of us who attended her first meeting. "I want you to think of something to do to get patients' minds off themselves. Any suggestions?" I had an idea, but I wouldn't share it.

I joined Scout's small group of volunteers, not quite sure what I would do. Each Tuesday morning I looked over the charts of patients assigned to me—then I visited with them.

Just talking was often hard for me, so I shared my idea with Scout. "I can paint a little. Maybe patients would like to paint."

Scout liked the idea. Before I could back out she was making a list of needed supplies. And soon I felt comfortable about running around the hospital with my arms full of paints and brushes while the others carried flowers, mail, and charts.

I loved the psychiatric division. I was amazed to learn that many nurses didn't want to work there. Alcoholics, suicidal young mothers, dope addicts, senile elderly people, acutely depressed individuals didn't frighten me. I felt only admiration for them. They had asked for help with a problem.

One of the first patients I met there was a young mother of six-month-old twin boys. "I can't do it any more," she sobbed. "Can you possibly understand what it's like when they both cry at the same time?"

I nodded and pulled out pictures of Jon and Jeremy.

44

On the surgical floor I cleaned blood and dirt from the toenails of a teenage girl as she assailed me with four-letter words. She was in a cast from her waist down. Everyone in the car, including her baby, had been killed instantly. There had been many men in her young and desperate life.

I wasn't sure I could give her the pedicure she asked for. She didn't think I could do it, either. But I thought about Jesus as he washed the feet of his disciples. I finished by painting her toenails bright red. Finally, I painted a picture of flowers on her cast.

"Lemme try them paints? Ain't it hard?" We looked through a book together for an idea of something she wanted to paint. She stopped looking when she came to the picture of a little bird watching over her babies. Slowly she read the poem under the picture. It was called "The Prayer of a Little Bird," and it began: "Dear God, I don't know how to pray by myself very well."

I hung her little bird painting on her traction bars. I wanted to stay longer with her, but I had others to visit. I left her reading *True Confessions* and glancing at the little bird she had painted.

One Tuesday I picked up my assignment sheet. It read: "Have Mr. Pritchett, Room 4012, paint a picture." I read his record. "Twenty-three years old. Paralyzed from the neck down for three years. Hospitalized for severe kidney problems. Depressed. Poor physical condition."

No way. Not me. I'm not going near him. I'm not even a real art teacher, much less one who can teach a totally paralyzed man to paint.

I quickly turned his chart over and decided to forget Mr. Pritchett. The next week his assignment was at the top of the list. It was underlined in red. Fear crawled up my neck. I'd been afraid so much. I didn't want to be afraid again. I wasn't going to see him. I wouldn't even go on the fourth floor.

The third week, I had only one assignment. In capital letters, "Marion, go and have Coy Pritchett paint a picture!!" What a time to remember my prayer: "God give me one person . . . anyone."

I gathered up my materials and started for the door marked "Stairs." I didn't like to ride the elevators. Didn't like to wait for

45

them and I figured the walking up and down stairs was good exercise. I walked slowly praying: "I'm scared, God. I don't want to go. Please let him be asleep. Or let him refuse to paint. Please. I don't know how to do this."

I stopped by the nurses' station of the fourth floor to get permission to enter his room. The station was busy with morning activity. Nurses, aides, and doctors jammed it.

"Excuse me." No one looked up. "Pardon me. I need to see a patient." Still no response. In a louder voice I asked, "May I have Mr. Pritchett paint a picture?"

All the activity stopped like a motion picture when the film sticks. Everyone looked at me. Then several nurses laughed. A doctor frowned over his glasses at me. The head nurse spoke: "Mr. Pritchett is paralyzed from the neck down. You have the wrong patient."

"I know he is. But he has been asigned to me."

She stared at me a moment longer. I stared back.

"Well, what's he going to paint with, his teeth?" she asked impatiently.

"Yes." She didn't know I had just grabbed her idea.

"You're wasting your time. Go ahead."

My heart was pounding. His door was closed. I knocked gently. *Maybe he's asleep. Oh, please God, let him be asleep.*

At the first soft rap I heard, "Come in."

There was nothing else to do. I opened the door praying as I entered, "Take over, God . . . You're on."

12

You Want to Paint?

I entered an incredibly small room and got my first look at a Stryker frame, a lightweight bed that rotates a patient who can't move. Coy was lying on his stomach looking down at the floor through the places where his face rested on the canvas. All I could see was the back of his head, and his heels that stuck out from under the sheet. There was a healing pressure sore on one heel. Out the window, inches away, a brick wall formed the "view." Immediately I was filled with anger. He needed something beautiful to look at.

I talked to the back of his head. "Hi, would you like to paint a picture?"

"Yes, I would." His answer was instant. A determination was born in me, and I knew he would do it.

"How do I get you turned over?"

"You have to get an orderly. It takes two of them to turn me."

One was hard enough to find . . . two almost impossible. "Be right back." I hurried from the room and spotted an orderly. "We have to get Mr. Pritchett turned over right away."

"Yes ma'am." He started toward the room. I wore a white jacket over my pink uniform to denote I was a recreational therapy worker. Maybe the orderly thought the white jacket meant more than it did. At any rate he assured me, "I'll get some help and get him turned over before you get back."

I ran down the four flights of stairs. I must have cardboard. Coy should have something hard to paint on. At Central Supply I spotted cardboard boxes containing surgical supplies. I opened one and found inside a piece of heavy cardboard. A hospital official came up and asked if he could help me. "I must have lots of cardboard." He began pulling out sheets of it for me and moving the heavy boxes.

"Thanks, this will do for right now. But save more for me."

"Right," he agreed.

I ran back up the stairs. Coy's door was open and I entered again and saw his face for the first time. "Hi."

"Hi," he smiled. *What a warm smile! No pain or bitterness—just gratitude.*

I didn't have time to feel sorry for him. I had to figure out how he was going to paint. As I got out the paint we began talking easily. He loved the woods and nature and animals. So I suggested he paint something he knew about. He told me about his mother's flowers. We settled on a single flower—a daisy.

I broke a brush in two and he almost shouted, "Hey, don't do

47

that for me. Those things cost money."

"I'll break all of them if we need to. They're too long for you."
I wrapped adhesive tape around the edges to make it smooth in
his mouth.

"Ready?" I asked.

"Ready as I'll ever be," he grinned.

I reached the brush toward his mouth. We both began to laugh.
I grabbed the brush back and held it, and we laughed until we
felt even more relaxed over what we were to attempt.

"We've got to be serious, now. I have to go in a little while."
I held the cardboard in front of his face. In a few minutes, holding
the brush with his teeth, he shook his head in protest. "You're holding
it too close . . . back up." It was hard for both of us. My back
ached, and sweat poured from his face. We had to stop often for
me to wipe his face with a towel.

Finally, it was finished. Neither of us said anything. I taped the
picture up on the wall. "What do you want to do next?" He laughed
out loud. "You got to be kidding, woman. I'm tired. I ain't doing
nothing else." But he began telling me about some rabbits he'd seen
once . . . a mother and two babies hiding under some leaves. I
stuck the brush in his mouth, and he started his second picture.
My legs and back and arms ached until I thought I'd have to stop
holding the cardboard for him. His face was pained now, and the
sheets were wet from his sweating. The flower had been good, but
this had a certain tenderness. A feeling of protection.

When he finished, he dropped his head back on the pillow, and
I wiped his face again and gave him something to drink. I put up
the second picture and flopped in a chair like Raggedy Ann. We
looked at the pictures silently.

"What are you so tired about? I did all the work," he complained,
grinning.

"You think it's easy holding a piece of cardboard and taking orders
from you? We'll do more next week. Be thinking about what you
want to paint."

"It'll take me a week to rest up. You always get what you want?"

"I've got to go. I have to pick up my boys at nursery school."

48

"You got kids?" He seemed very interested.

"Four."

"Lucky you . . . lucky kids, too. I'll bet you're a good mother."

A tinge of my fear returned. "I'm not! Really I'm not. It's hard, and I'm so impatient."

"Tell me. I saw what patience you got."

"Thank you." My fatigue evaporated. As much as I hated to leave Coy, I was suddenly anxious to see Jon and Jeremy.

As I passed the nurses' station I called out to the two busy nurses, "Hey, go and see Coy's pictures when you get a chance."

I opened the door to the stairs. Looking back over my shoulder, I saw the nurses running toward his room. Running, skipping, and jumping down the steps, I felt joy surge through me like a tidal wave.

13

Move This Mountain, Lord

It was hard waiting until Tuesday to paint with Coy. I began going to visit him on weekends. One Saturday before we started painting, Coy grinned, "Hey, I got this poem in my head. Could you write it down?" I wrote as he carefully dictated the poem. He seemed happy over releasing it. It's title: "The Love of God and a Friend." It told of Coy's accident. He had dived from a bridge and hit a floating log in the water. A cousin rescued him as he was sinking, already paralyzed.

I read it back to him and said I'd have copies made and bring them for him to give his friends. That was the beginning of a flood of poems, songs, and shared concerns.

"How's your kids?"

"Horrible."

"I got a son," he said proudly. "Ted. His mother took him right after the accident, and she don't want me to see him. But I'm supposed to see him every other weekend. She's married again. Ted wants to live with me and my folks. Maybe he can someday." He told me of the good days when he worked long hours on a construction job and came home to his family. His eyes shone as he remembered. "I took Ted hunting one day. His mama had a fit. He was so little. But I took him anyway. He learned good. He's a smart boy."

"Like his daddy," I smiled.

"I don't know about that," Coy joked back.

"How old is he?"

"Six."

He changed the conversation quickly. "Hey, you gonna make me paint today?" I pulled the little broken brush from my pocket and looked at it for a moment. I carried it all over the hospital with me. How many patients had I shown it to? Whenever someone complained or insisted he couldn't paint, I pulled out the little brush and told him why it was so short and wrapped in tape. And why it bore teeth marks.

Coy painted a bird eating red berries. He looked especially tired, and we stopped with one picture. He wanted to talk. "Most of my family don't come to see me. They tried. Really did. But when they got to that door I could feel them not wanting to come in. I know how people feel right away. My . . . condition never bothered you."

"I was too busy being scared that I might not teach you to paint. This is hardly my specialty." He still wanted to talk. "How did you ever accept it so well?"

He laughed. "I screamed for the first year. It didn't help none. God's got a plan for everyone . . . me, too. My life ain't much, but I'm gonna live it the best I can to honor him."

I had met Coy's parents. His daddy usually sat with him day and night. For weeks, sometimes months, he stayed at the hospital. It was a way of life for him. Coy was in and out of hospitals with kidney problems and viruses. Coy's daddy was in his seventies . . . and he looked tired. He always smiled at me, though. Then he would leave the room "to walk around a spell." Coy's mother stayed at home in Jefferson, about twenty miles from the hospital.

"Coy, your daddy is looking tired. Ask him to come home with me and take a break . . . and have supper with us. I'll bring him right back."

"I wish to God he would leave. You help me talk him into it."

Mr. Pritchett came into the room and gave me a quick, silent smile. Then he looked at Coy. Mr. Pritchett's overalls were wrinkled; his eyes tired; he needed a shave. He stood by Coy grinning down at him.

"Daddy, Mrs. West wants you to go home with her."

"I ain't a-going."

"Daddy, do it for me."

"Nope."

Coy looked at me and shook his head.

"Mr. Pritchett, Coy is worrying about you. Please come."

"Nope."

"Go on, Daddy," Coy shouted, near anger.

I wrote my telephone number down. "Come on, we'll give this to the nurse." He was a stubborn, shy, weary old man. He didn't want to meet my family. He didn't like strangers . . . and he didn't want to leave Coy. He was so exhausted he wavered a bit. I knew he'd been eating the food Coy left on his plate.

"You gon' bring me back soon's we eat?" he glared at me.

"I promise."

He took a comb from his overall pocket and stepped over to the sink to wet it and began combing his unruly hair. He buttoned the top button on his worn shirt and took his jacket off the hook. He went over to Coy and leaned over him, "You gon' be all right, Sugar Babe?"

"Daddy, you look so sharp, you might just forget to come back."

"Dad-gum it, son, I ain't a-going!"

"Daddy!"

"All right, Sugar Babe."

Thank you, Lord. You really do move mountains.

As we drove up in the yard, Jerry was cutting the grass. *Lord, let Jerry understand. Sometimes he doesn't when I do things like this.*

Jerry cut the lawn mower off, wiped his hands on his pants and came forward to stick out his hand. "You must be Mr. Pritchett. I'm glad you came. Marion's told us about you." He pulled up a lawn chair for Mr. Pritchett and himself, the grass forgotten. The children engulfed the old man. A twin sat on each knee and Julie and Jennifer stood by the chair, first on one foot, then another.

After a while I called them to supper. Mr. Pritchett looked a bit uneasy, and I showed him the bathroom. We waited for our guest in lovely silence that was a rarity at our house. As he sat down, slowly he reached out and touched Julie's red hair. "You got pretty hair, young 'un."

"Thank you," she smiled at him, then at me.

Jerry asked the blessing and we ate.

After the meal Mr. Pritchett stood up and thanked us. "If ya'll would ever come out to the house, we'd be proud to have you."

"Oh, we'd love to, Mr. Pritchett. Thank you."

Then he talked so much I couldn't believe it. He told us how serious Coy's kidney problem was and that the doctors couldn't do much for him. It became difficult for him to talk. "I got to be getting back. I thank you all."

Jerry and the girls drove him back, and I did the dishes. Jon and Jeremy pulled out pots and pans and fought. The house was a mess since I'd spent most of the afternoon at the hospital. Mud had been tracked through the den and peanut butter stuck on the wallpaper in the kitchen. Everyone had missed the overflowing garbage pail under the sink. I would have to wash clothes after the children were in bed. But I caught a glimpse of my reflection in the kitchen window. I was smiling. I felt the smile go down to my toes.

I was to recall this moment nearly four years later when I heard a minister say: "Dr. Karl Menninger was asked if there was a way to avoid a breakdown if a person realized he was heading for one. Dr. Menninger replied that there was, but it was so simple very few people would try it.

" 'What is it?' asked the man questioning Dr. Menninger.

"Dr. Menninger replied, 'The person about to have a breakdown should walk out his front door and find someone who needs help . . . anyone . . . and help him.' "

14

A Rose for Me

The next week I went out early one morning to get the paper before anyone was awake. I stood in the dew-soaked grass looking at the front page in amazement. There was a large picture of Coy and his parents. His painting of the red bird eating the berries was on the Stryker frame with Coy. The long article with several pictures on the following page told of Coy's situation, his accident, his wife's abandonment, and his aged parent's tireless efforts to care for him. He was hailed as an artist.

Joy overflowed in tears. But my excitement didn't match Coy's when I saw him. His success spurred us both to new areas of happiness. When Coy dictated more poems I suggested, "Hey, you could write these yourself."

"Huh?"

"I'll bet you could type better than I can."

He laughed out loud, but I knew if he had the chance, he'd try. Scout thought he could too.

Several times the doctors didn't think Coy would make it. He would be rushed back to the hospital. When I'd call Mrs. Pritchett, she'd say: "It's bad, Mrs. West. Pray. Pray hard." Often Coy would stubbornly shut his eyes and refuse to eat. Hospital personnel soon became irritated with this performance. If he got improper treatment, he retreated by closing his eyes and not speaking. One morning I went in to learn that an orderly had dropped Coy during the night as he turned him. I went to Coy's room.

His daddy sat as close to him as he could get. The sheet was pulled over Coy's face. I stood for a moment looking horrified. Mr. Pritchett explained, "Coy's asleep. He likes the sheet over his face when he's . . . like this."

I pulled it down. His fluttering eyelids told me he wasn't asleep. He wouldn't respond to my pleas or threats.

A nurse came in with orderlies and told Coy he was going out into the sun. Ordinarily this was a rare treat. Outside, in the bright sun, he kept his eyes closed.

"It's a beautiful day, Coy. Open your eyes." They remained tightly closed.

I ran across the street and got him a big orange drink. I knew how much he loved them. I put the straw to his lips. They seemed to seal even tighter. I took the straw out and tried to pour some into his mouth. It ran down his face. Finally they took him back inside.

A nurse told me, "He's got to drink something. Keep trying." I tried for nearly an hour. I walked to the door of his room with my arms folded and looked out into the hall. "Lord, I don't know what to do. I have to go home. Isn't there anyone who can get through to him?"

Just then I saw Jim Griffith, our pastor, coming down the hall. He knew about Coy but hadn't met him. I quickly explained the situation to him. "Will you try to get him to drink something?"

"I'll try," Dr. Griffith smiled. In a few minutes he came out smiling and handed me the empty orange drink cup. "He said, would you get him another one?"

I hurried back into Coy's room, and he was grinning as if the whole thing hadn't happened. I stood with my hands on my hips glaring at him. He laughed. "You are the only person I have ever met who's as stubborn as me. I like your preacher, too."

His paintings were all around his room . . . nine of them. One day I gathered them all up and took them to an expert framer. I told him how they had been painted. He knew what I wanted before I asked. And he agreed to frame them . . . free.

"I don't know how to thank you," I said, amazed that I'd asked such a thing of him. "I want to do it." His eyes shone.

In a few days I stopped by to pick them up. I wasn't prepared for what he had done. They were breathtaking. The owner admired them with me. I hurried back to the hospital with them. A nurse helped me carry them to Coy's room. She told me before we got there. "He's having a bad day . . . lots of pain." I could feel his agony hanging in the room as we entered. I got down on my hands and knees and looked up in his face. He was on the Stryker frame, face down. His face was twisted in silent pain that made me want to run away . . . out into the sunshine.

"Bad?" I asked. He didn't answer.

"Can I show you something?"

"What if I said no?"

"I'd show you anyway."

"I figured."

I spread the pictures out on the floor under his face. He knew I'd taken them away . . . but he thought I was going to show them to someone.

As he grinned down at them, a tear dropped by one of the paintings. I walked out of the room and left him with his work.

The volunteer group I had originally joined bought four of the pictures and hung them in the pediatric section. They were hung across from the room Rosemary had been in.

Hilda, my next door neighbor, had now joined the Pink Ladies and had come into the recreational therapy program. She printed in Old English script Coy's story and how the paintings were done. This too was framed and hung with the pictures. Several other people bought his paintings. Contributions were coming in from people who read about Coy. He wouldn't accept the money from the paintings so Scout handled it for him. It wasn't nearly enough, and I don't know where the rest came from, but one day Scout and I went to Coy's room and presented him with an electric typewriter, a camera (he had wanted pictures of hospital personnel), and a complete set of art supplies.

And when he went home a new Stryker frame went with him.

He was sitting in his wheel chair when we entered with the gifts. His daddy was out of the room. I stuck a pencil in his mouth. Slowly he typed COY T. PRITCHETT. I looked out at the brick wall and quickly wiped away my tears. Scout was able to hold hers inside, and Coy's fell onto the typewriter.

I hurried home and printed a large replica of a typewriter keyboard. Then rushed back to the hospital to tape it on the ceiling. Hilda went with me to hold the ladder. I knew he'd have it memorized in no time. As I climbed up on the ladder with the tape in my mouth he called out, "Hey, don't fall on me. That's all I need. You and the ladder falling on me." He began studying the chart even before I climbed down. Soon he was able to type his own poems and letters.

When Coy was released from the hospital I told him I'd like to come see him. He told me how to get to his house and said he hoped I'd bring the children and Jerry. Then he added, "You'll never come."

Julie and Jennifer had been allowed to visit him. They had shown old home movies and done skits for him. His laughter had filled the halls. We wanted Jerry to meet him. Jerry felt about hospitals like I did football games—the further away they were, the better. I hinted all one Sunday how nice it would be if he took Coy some homemade ice cream. "I'll go with you and feed him, Daddy," Julie offered. He refused and stormed out of the room. "I think he's going to go, Mama. Let's pray . . . cause you know how he hates hospitals."

After a while Jerry walked back into the kitchen looking grim. "Where's the ice cream?" he growled at me. Julie did a little victory dance behind his back as I got the ice cream ready.

Nearly two hours passed before they returned. They both came in smiling and Julie volunteered, "Daddy was great, Mama. Coy liked him better than anybody. They watched the ball game together and talked about sports. He was real depressed until Daddy got there."

"He's just tired of all you women around him," Jerry insisted, but he had a look of very special happiness about him.

I missed seeing Coy at the hospital, but I became involved with many other patients. I stopped to talk to the young girl who had painted the little bird. Nearly three months had passed, and she was about to be dismissed. Now she sat out in the hall and greeted everyone that came by. She hardly seemed like the same person.

"About time for you to go home, isn't it?" I called out to her.

"Yes, but do you know what? I want to come back here. I want to be a nurse's aide. Do you think I can do that? I want to help people."

"Oh, yes . . . you can do it. I know you can. Hurry back."

"I will," she grinned. "I'll be back soon. You'll see."

There were many patients . . . but Coy remained the one person I had prayed God would give me.

One day a few weeks after he had gone home with his parents, I found a letter in my mailbox. I didn't recognize the typing. But as soon as I unfolded the sheet of typing paper, I recognized the artist.

It was a picture of a perfect, single, red rose, with thorns and a bud. It leaned a little to the left, so lifelike. At the top it read: "For Marion and Julie."

Standing at the mailbox I laughed and cried. Coy had painted without my help.

15

Do You Believe in Miracles?

It was Jerry's suggestion. "Let's ride out to see Coy today." It had been months since Coy had gone home from the hospital. The beautiful sunny Sunday afternoon made us all want to go somewhere.

I thought I knew how to get to Coy's house. We made several turns I felt were right. Suddenly I saw the enormous, old oak tree.

"That's it," I screamed. "There's the old oak tree he's told me about. That's the one his pet owl lives in."

When we turned into the driveway we saw a ramp instead of steps leading up to the front porch. We learned later that their church had built it. Containers of many sizes on the porch held thriving green plants and flowers. The small, humming air conditioner that overhung the front porch seemed almost out of place protruding from the worn weather-beaten home.

Mrs. Pritchett, surprised and pleased, let us in. She loved for Coy to have visitors. His bed was inches from the door. Over in a corner I saw his new Stryker frame. I knew what a tremendous help this was to the Pritchetts.

Coy got his first look at Jon and Jeremy. They crawled up on the bed and sat on him. As I attempted to get them down Coy stopped me, "Leave them alone. Hey fellers. Y'all give your Mama a hard time?"

They both started to talk to him at once. We sat down in the small room and began talking. Pictures, artificial flowers, and mementos covered the walls and tables. Mrs. Pritchett went back to the kitchen, and I followed her. Her hair was brushed back from her round face. Her large upper arms flapped constantly as she talked. I couldn't stop looking at her eyes . . . laughing eyes. She still had laughing eyes and a keen sense of humor.

The three-room home was immaculately clean and scrubbed. Coy's mother showed me several projects. She was covering a chair and planned to put new linoleum in Coy's room.

After that, we went often. A small group of us from Beech Haven Baptist Church went one night and had an ice cream party. We sang. Coy had a good voice and loved country music. Mr. Pritchett's solemn expression never changed . . . just like we weren't there. But Mrs. Pritchett's entire face now matched her laughing eyes, and she stood in the doorway patting her foot and clapping her hands in time to the music.

They had us for supper one night. We ate in shifts since there were only four chairs. The sweet potato casserole broke in the oven, and it looked so good I scooped out some and ate it, anyway. Mrs. Pritchett laughed until she cried.

After four months of visits, the boys were dismissed from the Rutland Center. Jon had quieted down and seemed to have stopped copying Jeremy. Just before we left he told me after one of their group play sessions with other children: "Mama, did you see that new boy. Well, he has the same problem I had. Did you see how he acted? I hope he gets better . . . like me." Jon wasn't quite three. And it was Jon, after we were dismissed from the Center, who came up to me one day as I sat in the yard. He handed me a flower and said softly, "My real Mama has come back."

I knew the sessions between Mrs. Levine and me were coming

to an end. Much of what I had to talk about now were the plusses in my life.

One of those first plusses toward the beginning of the sessions was very special. "We're fixing up the boys' room again," I told her. From my descriptions she knew that it looked like a disaster area. The twins' precocious activity had knocked out the screens and pulled down the curtains. Because they turned over the furniture, we removed most of it. The walls were scarred and soiled. Empty closets and a homemade chicken-wire cage with a lock on it on top of Jeremy's bed gave the room a hopeless air.

Mrs. Levine clapped her hands saying, "Wonderful. Tell me about what you're doing."

I thought the most exciting part was the mural I was painting on the boys' closet doors. It was of a circus with a small village in the background. A train passed through and an airplane flew overhead. A little white church with a steeple nestled in some trees. Jon and Jeremy stood just outside a small white picket fence, watching children at the circus. Their footprints in the dusty road behind them showed they had just arrived. At the bottom I signed "For Jon and Jeremy, September, 1970." It was much more than a picture to me . . . it was a promise. A promise that things were going to be different for them and for me.

Mrs. Levine also knew how my work with Coy had helped me. One day I shared my fear for him: "Coy's not doing well at all. His kidneys are failing. And he's so brave and uncomplaining. Some other patients with minor ailments whine all the time, but he never complains."

She listened and directed the conversation to my daddy's death. He had died when he was just a few years older than Coy. He died with strep throat because penicillin wasn't available in 1938. I knew Mrs. Levine thought I was associating the two. Maybe I was . . . I didn't know. But I knew I was getting close to tears, and I'd never cried in her office.

"If he can accept his fate, why can't you, Mrs. West?" she asked with compassion.

"Don't you believe in miracles?" I asked beginning to feel more like I might cry.

"No," she answered softly.

I wanted to beg her, *Please believe in miracles. They still happen. You must believe they do.* But I said nothing. Her answer released the tears in me, and I sat and cried. She assumed I was crying for Coy and for my father. And I guess I was. But some of my tears were for her . . . I wanted her to believe in miracles.

Near Christmas she said I could stop coming. I had expected it and was ready for it. We had one more visit scheduled before Christmas. I knew what I wanted to give her, but couldn't decide how to wrap it. Do you put Christmas paper on a gift for a Jewish friend? And what do you say when you hand it to her? I decided on gold paper with a gold cord. And I would say, "Here . . . this is for you."

The gift turned out just like I wanted. I did a miniature painting of a mother and two little boys with red hair. They were walking in a field of daisies. Facial expressions didn't show, but somehow there was a feeling of joy and freedom in the picture. As I got up to leave from that last visit, I took it out of my purse. "This is for you."

She seemed surprised. Then it was my turn to be surprised. She began opening it with me still there watching. She looked at it for a long time. Then said, "Thank you." There were tears in her eyes. I left quickly because I felt tears coming in mine.

As I left the old house for the last time I thought: *she was crying! Somehow her tears made her dearer to me. She must have liked the gift . . . and understood it. And I wonder if she won't think sometime that what has happened to me is a miracle. She was part of a miracle in my life.*

16

I Care!

Wow, I'm tired. Supper finished, I thought of staying home, but Jerry offered to do the dishes. Although he didn't understand this obsession I had about hospitals, he encouraged me to go. I was doing volunteer work at two hospitals now. It was my night to work at St. Mary's in the emergency room.

Almost reluctantly, I dressed. But as soon as I entered the swinging doors and the hospital smell, I wasn't tired any more.

About 9:30 an ambulance came wailing in. "An overdose," someone said. I stood back while the doctor and nurses worked with him. After a while they asked me to sit and watch him.

"Please help him, God." After a while he began to mumble. "Bill," I called his name softly. They hadn't told me to do anything except sit with him. No one had said I could talk to him.

"Lemme alone."

"Bill, can you hear me?"

Suddenly he sobbed, "Nobody cares . . . nobody cares." Deep sobs racked his body. "Bill," I said loudly, not caring who heard me, "I care. I care, Bill!"

He opened his eyes for a moment. Tears slid down his face, and I wiped them out of his ears with the sheet. "You're just saying that."

"No I'm not. I don't have to sit here with you. I'm a volunteer. I'm here because I want to be." I looked at my watch. It was after eleven. "It's way past time for me to go home. I wanted to stay here with you."

He curled into an embryo position and cried.

I repeated: "I care, Bill. I really do."

Near midnight I knew I must go home. Bill was to be admitted. I didn't want to leave. Who was going to talk with him and listen to him? I asked an intern if he would.

"He needs professional help. We can't help him."

"But you can care."

"Best not to get involved."

I looked at Bill once more and asked God to watch over him and send someone to him.

I thought about Bill all through the next day. I tried to push the thoughts away. *Don't get involved.* By five o'clock the desire to go see him was pulling at me like a magnet. I'll just call, I decided.

The emergency room nurse told me his room number, but said he couldn't have visitors. "Wheew," I sighed. "Okay."

"Wait . . . if you wear your uniform I believe you can get in."

Jerry and I planned to go out at 7:30. It was then 5:00. Traffic was at its worst, and I was cooking supper. The boys fought in front of the television.

Go see him. The thought was powerful. *They won't let me in. How do you know? I don't have time. It won't take long. I don't know what to say to him.*

I looked out my kitchen window and saw a few late blooming flowers. Just enough for a bouquet. *You could take those and not say anything. Lord, I'm serious. If the phone rings within three minutes, I'm on my way. I'll know this pull to go is from you.*

I stared at the phone and jumped as its loud shrill sent a shiver up my spine. It was a routine reminder of a meeting at church for Julie. As I took the message, I began taking off my tennis shoes and unbuttoning my blouse.

"Julie," I called out as I slipped into my Red Cross uniform, "Can you watch supper and keep the boys from fighting?"

"Mama . . ." she began a protest. Quickly I explained the situation, and her attitude changed to "Hurry Mama, hurry."

I snatched the flowers from the yard and drove off. At an intersection I hit a traffic jam. *Lord, move those cars over. Clear me a path. You moved the Red Sea. Move a few cars.* The way opened up, and I slipped through. I glanced in the rear view mirror to see it was closed again.

As I got off the elevator on Bill's floor I realized I'd forgotten his room number. I stood perplexed. A head sister came up to me and smiled. She waited for me to say something. "I came to see

Bill. I forgot the number. I know he can't have visitors," I said.

She put her large arm around me, saying how lovely the flowers were as she guided me to his room. "Thank you for coming, dear," she said.

A young man stood by Bill's bed. "There she is," Bill shouted as I entered the room. "I've been waiting all day. I knew you would come back." To his friend he said, "She's the lady I was telling you about . . . the lady that cared."

"Bill, I didn't think you'd remember last night."

"I remembered you cared."

The visitor left. I sat on Bill's bed and began telling him that God had a plan for his life and that He cared about Bill more than he could imagine. I wasn't sure Bill believed me, but he sure listened. He wiped his tears away on the bed sheet. When I invited him to go to church with us and come for a meal, he accepted right away.

Then a man rushed into the room and embraced Bill. I said to him: "Whoever you are, I'm so glad you're here." Bill happily introduced his brother. The brother had been searching for Bill for more than a week since Bill had run away from home. He lived nearly a thousand miles away.

Out in the hall, Bill's brother told me he wanted Bill to come home voluntarily.

"I'll pray he will," I said.

I went back to see Bill two more times. On my last visit he told me, "I'm going back home with my brother. I need help. I know I do." *You've come a long way . . . when you can say that.*

I asked friends to pray for Bill. My Sunday School class prayed for him. My family did, too.

Months later I received a card from Bill. Things were going well. His family also wrote me. I answered his card, and at Christmas he wrote again.

Could it have just been chance that Bill and I met? Had God really used me?

Someone shared a book with me. A passage caught my eye. It stated that God looks down and sees people in need and people

willing to help, and He is continually trying to get them together.
Thank you, Lord, for Bill and that I was there to care about him.

17

It Just Can't Be

"Marion," Sue Turner, one of my mother's closest friends, was calling. From the tone of her voice I prepared for bad news. "How are the boys?"

The twins were not yet three weeks old. "Fine, Sue."

Is it my mother or Big, dear God . . . which one?

Big was my stepfather . . . nearly fifty years older than I and twenty years older than my mother. His real name was Henry, but those who loved him best affectionately called him Big. He had a sharp sense of humor that age and sickness were trying to take away from him, but he hung on . . . especially when the children were around.

"Marion, Big is sick. They've taken him to Greenville, South Carolina. Your mother is with him in the ambulance. He had a stroke or something, but he managed to get to the phone and call your mother at the bank. I believe they will operate right away from what the doctors here said. She wanted me to call you. And she said to tell you that she is just fine."

I knew she was, too. She would be taking it as it came, smiling, thanking anyone who helped them. Speaking softly.

"Thank you, Sue. Thank you so much for calling."

Big was in surgery for nearly seven hours, and my mother waited through the night. He had suffered a severe aneurysm. The surgery involved opening his chest and both legs. When it was over the doctor told my mother, "I did all I could. It's up to God now." My mother kissed the doctor's hands.

When she called me she sounded grateful, hopeful, and calm. But for a week, everytime the phone rang, I thought: This may be it.

He's gone.

As Jerry and I got up to feed the babies during the night, I prayed. Throughout the day I prayed. "God, I don't think Big's going to heaven. Please give us another chance. I've passed up so many chances to talk to him. Don't take him now. A little longer please."

He was transferred to their hometown in Elberton, Georgia. But he seemed to have lost the will to live. He was seventy-eight years old and very tired. The doctors said it was a matter of time for him.

He had never seen Jon and Jeremy. I knew it wasn't practical to take the twins to see him. They were just a few weeks old. How could I get them into his hospital room? I had to try. Jerry agreed, and Edna said she could go with us.

Mother said she would try to have someone at the back door to let us in. She thought the hospital would give permission. When we drove up to the back door, Margaret Powell, a friend of ours who worked there, met us. As we got on the elevator with the babies and Julie and Jennifer, several hospital personnel told us we couldn't come in with all the children. But Margaret told them it had all been approved.

We went to Big's room. He was so weak and sick I hardly recognized him. He didn't seem to know me. Trying to be natural, I kissed him. Then we put a baby in each of his arms. He struggled up and held them protectively. Then he threw his head back and laughed out loud. He began talking to them and adjusting the little receiving blankets around them. I told him which one was named for him. He called Julie and Jennifer over and began talking to them like he always had. An orderly shook his head in disbelief and grinned at Mother. She was smiling and making an effort not to cry. Right before our eyes Big seemed to regain his will to live.

Two years later he and mother were visiting us. He had a bad spell and couldn't breathe. Julie, watching, was obviously terrified. This could be it, I thought. But he recovered.

Another two years later Julie came to me one night. "Mother, I promised God if he wouldn't let Big die that day he got so sick at our house, I'd tell him how to be saved . . . in case he's not. I haven't done it. Mama, do you think Big's saved?"

"No, Julie. I don't think so."

"Well, when I was sitting in the bathtub tonight I think God reminded me of that promise. Can God talk to you in the bathtub?"

"He talks to me there."

"I believe he's told me something to write to Big. Is it all right if I write to him? Do you think it'll make him mad?"

"I don't think so, but you must write it, Julie."

She handed me the letter when she was finished. I read it through tears.

DEAR BIG,

How are you feeling? I felt such a strong urge to write you this letter.

A few years ago, on the boys' birthday you and "Goge" and "Westie" and "Daddy Robert" were over at our house. You got sick. I prayed that if God would spare you I would tell you the plan of salvation. I promised it to God.

This is my favorite verse in the Bible. "For God so loved the world that he gave his only begotton son, that whosoever believeth in him should not perish, but have everlasting life."

Big, God loves you. He loves you *so very much* that he let his own son die on the cross for you. I know it seems like there is a wall between you and God. There is. The Bible says there is. This wall is SIN. The Bible says that all have sinned and come short of the glory of God. When Jesus died on the cross, He took with him the sins of the world, so that we might live forever. But He also arose. Jesus is living today. He *will* help you. But only if you ask. Ask and it shall be given you, seek and you shall find, knock and the door shall be opened unto you. For everyone that asketh receiveth, and he that knocketh it shall be opened unto you.

I love you, Big. I'm praying for you.

Your granddaughter,
JULIE

My mother told me later that Big read the letter over and over with his magnifying glass. He kept it in his mother's Bible.

One day while we visited them in Elberton, he and I were alone in the yard. He rubbed his feet. They hurt almost constantly now, and walking was very difficult for him. He looked at me and said,

"I want to die in that bedroom in there." He pointed to the house.

"I know," I said.

"Will you try to see that I do?"

"I'll try." After a little silence I asked, "What about after that?"

"What do you mean?"

"Where do you want to go after that?"

"Won't matter then."

"Yes it will. Don't you want to go to heaven?"

"How do you know there is a heaven?"

"How do you know there isn't?"

He didn't answer, but looked away from me. I didn't want to argue with him. I pulled a "Four Spiritual Laws" booklet out of my pocket. "May I read a little booklet to you?"

He put on his glasses, "Yes."

I began reading from the booklet that explained salvation. "God loves you, and has a wonderful plan for your life . . ."

He listened closely until I got to the part about inviting Jesus into his heart.

Then he took off his glasses, screwed his face into a hard frown, and raised his voice: "It just can't be, Marion. It can't be. One God can't look down and see everyone of us. It's impossible. Besides, I don't believe in the virgin birth."

I shut the booklet and put it in his shirt pocket. Then I kissed him and whispered, "I love you."

The little booklet went into the Bible with Julie's letter. He read them both often.

And I continued praying, "Please, God, show him it can be."

18

Our House Is Too Small

The boys were three and a half. Jon's tonsils had to come out. I trusted God to take care of him. Even when the operation became more than routine because of the swollen condition of his tonsils and Jon's allergic reaction to a drug, I didn't worry. I felt concern, but not that panicky kind of worry that eats away at you.

Everytime the boys had a birthday Jerry reminded me: "Almost got it made, Mannie. They'll soon be in school."

Big's health was failing fast, but sometimes he had a good day. Mother continued to work at the bank. I was glad we lived only forty miles from them. We tried to go see them often. Sometimes he would make the tremendous effort to come to see us. Jerry's parents brought him and Mother. No matter how bad he felt, the children always brought a smile to his face.

"Supper's ready," I called one night. The twins came first, climbing up in their outgrown highchairs. Julie and Jennifer squeezed in between the table and the wall. Jerry and I sat at each end. It was like eating in a nice-sized closet. The twins sat so close to the other wall that they touched the wallpaper with their sticky hands. Often spilled milk sloshed down either wall.

"We've got to have more space," Jerry said. We all agreed. We had outgrown our house. We had discussed enclosing the carport or patio, but besides being too small, the house needed repairs. "The carpet needs replacing," I'd sigh. "Then the inside needs painting."

"And the wallpaper in the kitchen is yukkie," the girls would remind us.

Countless other repairs popped into my mind. All of this would be quite expensive. We wondered whether we should attempt this or just wait for Jerry's transfer that would probably come soon. We didn't want to redo the house if we were about to move. Should we consider buying another house in Athens? We looked at a larger house under construction nearby.

Everytime I cleaned the house, the problem of size bothered me more. The girls' closet was packed with clothes. I had saved some of their school papers since first grade, but I began throwing them out. I got rid of several small tables that I loved because of lack of space. The girls continued to argue and beg for more bedroom space. It seemed to me there were children everywhere . . . all the time.

Dreams of a new, larger home enslaved my mind. The most wonderful room in my dreamhouse was the playroom, a large room with red carpeting and wood paneling and low windows. With the playroom came four bedrooms and two . . . no, three bathrooms. Avocado carpeting on most of the floors blended with the avocado theme of the kitchen . . . a tremendous kitchen.

I began to hate my little house . . . even neglect it and envy people with larger houses. I hated being crowded. There wasn't even enough room in the den for everyone to sit. When one of us got up, another one grabbed the seat. "Please show us what to do, Lord."

I realized I had been so busy telling God about our needs for a larger house that I hadn't been listening to him. I remembered that he never shouts, but speaks in that still, small voice. I listened. Then I tried to ignore what I thought I heard. But the message didn't change.

You and Jerry, bring your requests to me together in prayer.

I remembered when we lost an important key. "It's supposed to be in this drawer!" Jerry had shouted. "Who took it?"

As both twins blamed the other one, we searched for the key. I pulled out the cushions on the sofa, and a gentle thought prodded me. *Why don't you pray? Of course. God, please help us find that key.*

No. Both of you pray.

About a key?

Is it important to you?

Oh, yes! We have to have it.

Then ask me for it . . . together.

I put the pillows back on the sofa and called out to Jerry who was searching in our bedroom, "Are you praying?"

"No, I'm looking."

"Well, I think we both need to pray. I am."

After a few moments came, "Me, too."

And then a shout like an Indian. Jerry walked into the den with his hand open for me to see. He and I stared down at the missing key.

"Where was it?"

"You won't believe it."

"Try me."

"In my drawer in the brown box, where it was supposed to be."

"But you looked there."

"I know."

You mean the same principle that works for a key works for a house . . . or anything, Lord?

Exactly.

I became positive that God wanted Jerry and me to pray together. Not in our family devotion time, but just the two of us.

God added a P.S. *Don't suggest this. Let Jerry do it.*

But you told me, and I want to get on with it.

I told him, too.

Really?

I decided to remain silent.

One night, somehow, we got all the children to bed a little early. We sat alone watching television in the den. I wanted so much to pray. I felt like standing in front of the television and shouting, "Let's pray." We'd never prayed before—just the two of us.

Instead I prayed, "Help me keep quiet, Lord." I looked at Jerry. He didn't seem to be concentrating on the screen. He looked at me suddenly, and I looked away quickly, afraid he could read my mind.

"Mannie, do you think we could pray about the house?"

My heart leaped. *Thank you, Lord.* "Oh, yes," I whispered.

Gratitude flooded through me, and tears slipped down my face. We were giving the problem to God. I knew he took it. And it wasn't our problem anymore.

19

Thank You, Anyway

I was going to get my new house. I felt it as surely as one feels spring in the air. Again and again I reminded God I wanted it to be his way . . . but chosen from my options . . . a sort of multiple choice, Plan A, B, or C. Any of them suited me. The end result of each of them was a new house.

I took back the request we'd given God as I decided exactly how God would answer the prayer. An opening became available in a nearby town with Jerry's company. Several company wives called me and said they had heard Jerry was the one to get the job . . . which meant a transfer, which naturally meant a new house! God had chosen my Plan B. Like visions of sugar plums, thoughts of our new house danced around in my head.

Thank you, God. This is just great! How wonderful it is to trust you. Why doesn't everyone do this? It's fun trusting you.

The telephone interrupted my happy thoughts. *Maybe it'd be a close friend. I could tell her about our upcoming move. No, better not tell anyone yet. Not until it's official. Jerry wouldn't like that.*

"Hello," I answered cheerfully. "Marion," Jerry's voice told me right away something was wrong. I felt like someone had hit me in the stomach. Jerry almost never called home during the day . . . unless it was for something special—like, "Did you take my suit to the cleaners?" or "I forgot to tell you. I've got a meeting tonight."

He wasn't saying anything special. He was just sort of making conversation. Very unlike him. I wanted to blurt out, "What's wrong?" But I didn't. Maybe it was my imagination. Then he told me quickly, like it was an afterthought. "Someone else got the job, Mannie." Immediately, he sounded better . . . happier. He said nice things about the man who got the job we thought was his. He was sincere. "See you tonight. Love you."

No move? No new house? I hung up thinking, "There must be some mistake. God is with us. He's on our side. We are supposed

71

to get a new house. This isn't my plan B at all." God hadn't chosen Plan A or C either . . . none of them. He had rejected all my plans.

I walked to the middle of the den. I felt hurt, anger, jealousy, resentment, and disappointment swooping down on me like giant hawks. They were going to tear me apart. I fled from them.

I knew that all my life I had really wanted my own way. It wasn't just the new house anymore. I had to give up all of me. I knew if I didn't, I would still try to tell God what to do . . . and live with bitterness and the things that tore me apart.

I wanted peace. I was standing at the brink of a decision I could no longer delay. It was like I was going to jump off a cliff, having been told someone waited to catch me.

Someone has said prayer is an attitude of the heart. I came to understand those words that afternoon in my den. My heart cried out, "I don't care what it costs. It doesn't matter anymore. I want you in total control of my life, no matter what happens. Take the last 5 percent of me that I've held back. I give it to you now. Forgive my dishonest prayer. Do it your way. But more than that, I want you to do *everything* your way in my life. I've called you Lord, but I haven't let you be Lord. As of this moment, I'm trusting you to be my Lord."

I was giving up the new house, and while I was giving it up I felt compelled to give myself up, too. It was a definite experience of surrender.

God heard the thoughts of my heart. My audible prayer of relinquishment, however, was only three words, "Thank you, anyway."

As I whispered it, I felt like shouting . . . maybe I did. "Thank you, oh, thank you!" I felt an outpouring of love that wouldn't stop . . . it washed over me. God poured more and more love on me.

This is the sweetest thing I have ever known in my life. You have told me "no" and given me all this love, too. Thank you. Thank you for telling me no! Thank you for loving me.

As the Holy Spirit filled me there in my den, I accepted myself as a new person and was amazed to realize how much I *liked* myself. It was not just a special prayer of closeness to the Lord.

I had surrendered to Christ when I was nine years old. Then I gave him all of me I knew to give. The next day . . . and the next year there was more of me and of my will. More that I did not surrender. Many years of me were in control by the time I was an adult. Jesus had been my Savior, but not my Lord.

As that child of nine I had been given a beautiful gift that I received . . . but just didn't open. I carried it around with me. At the age of thirty-three I opened the gift and found abundant life. What God intended for me I had kept wrapped up in lack of trust. The next day and the next and for all my days I would live and *daily* trust him and give each new day to him, but now I just loved him.

This new love was so wonderfully sweet that whenever I strayed away from complete trust I would feel compelled to come running back . . . to the fullness of *his* love.

I had never experienced such an outpouring of love. It just wouldn't stop coming . . . and it was for me! He kept on giving me more love, and right away I wanted to share it. All this love for me. I couldn't believe it was for me . . . but I knew it was. I received it.

All the old hymns I had sung as a child and even as an adult poured through my mind, and I understood them for the first time. I think I gasped when I realized that the people who had written them had experienced what I had . . . God's love. They were more than mere rhymes.

"Amazing grace, how sweet the sound," "At the cross, at the cross, where I first saw the light." "Nothing but the blood," "Jesus, Jesus, Jesus, sweetest name I know," "I surrender all," "Just as I am," "Have thine own way, Lord, Thou are the potter, I am the clay," . . . and the song I especially loved, "Out of my bondage, sorrow and night."

I thought, it's real . . . this thing I've heard about total surrender, it's real! I thought joyfully of people whom I knew had given up totally. And sadly, I thought of others, still struggling, having given Jesus only partial control.

I thought of those who were without him at all. And I wanted to run and start knocking on doors, like Paul Revere, asking "Do you know him? He's real, all right. He's who he says he is, and he loves you."

We must tell everybody that it's real. We must tell everyone that here is the secret of life and happiness . . . here is the answer to every problem. Here is another way to live. We must tell people. Why isn't it in the headlines and on the news?

Then sadly, I realized that's what Christians have been trying to do for centuries. Hadn't I myself missed this exciting total surrender to Jesus up until this very moment? Ministers had preached over and over to me, "Surrender yourself totally to Jesus. Get off the fence," and I felt myself freeze to those words . . . thinking: Oh, they need missionaries again, or a big job at the church needs filling." *You can't surrender fully to Jesus and just be a mother and wife. Anyway, if you could, who would want to live such a goodie-goodie life? You certainly wouldn't. That's not for you. Don't consider what he's saying for a moment. He's talking to someone else.*

Hadn't friends talked to me about total surrender? Didn't I hear it taught? Hadn't I read about it?

And hadn't I convinced myself that I had done it, refusing to listen to that still, small voice that insisted, "There's a little bit more of you to give. That little bit makes all the difference."

I was different. I knew I was. I ran to the mirror, leaned forward, and looked at my face.

I was beaming! I stood smiling at myself in the mirror, not even wiping away the tears and saying, "Thank you, Lord, thank you for loving me."

Suddenly, I loved my little crowded house with the worn wallpaper, soiled carpet, and walls covered with nicks and fingerprints.

I walked outside and looked up at the blue sky. I thought: I don't have a single problem or guilt or worry. God has taken them all. I am going to trust him in everything all my life.

20

A Time to Shut Up

Jerry came home that night, probably expecting a long-faced wife to greet him. Instead he found me happy and smiling. Throughout supper I didn't mention that our house was too small or that we weren't moving. He looked a bit puzzled, but I just kept smiling at him. I really didn't know how to explain what had happened.

As I got ready for bed that night I realized the date, March 4, 1972. Early that afternoon I "gave up," asking God to be in control of my life. It was four years to the date and almost to the minute from the time I had come home from the hospital with the twins, confident I could manage them, Julie and Jennifer, my husband, and my home.

Thank you, Lord, that I nearly fell apart . . . that the twins drove me up the wall. Thank you I had to sit here with them day after day and finally got a real good look at myself and my life. Thank you for working in my life.

I was so happy I could hardly sleep or eat. I just grinned at everybody and everything. I was conscious of Jerry watching me out of the corner of his eye. One night he asked, "Why don't you go ahead and see about the new carpeting and wallpaper and decide what color you want the inside painted?" I had hinted, then begged for this for nearly a year.

"It's okay, really. It's not bothering me. I'm happy." I didn't tell him that I was so busy talking with people about Jesus that I hardly had time to notice the house. Many days I spent hours on the phone or with people talking about Jesus and what he'd done in my life.

Some had surrendered their lives, and we talked about what a difference it made. Others were seeking a relationship with him. Somehow as I talked with anyone the subject of Jesus came up.

The days hardly seemed long enough. And I couldn't wait for the next one. I could barely remember the days I had been afraid to face. I was reading sometimes a book a day . . . spiritual books.

And I read my Bible with my mouth open in awe. I thought Ephesians was the most wonderful thing I'd ever read. And it had been in my Bible all the time. Incredible!

Bobby Leverett told me one day, "Marion, I've never seen anyone change so rapidly as you have. You ve been on a mountaintop for so long. Watch out. You'll have to come down soon. Don't go on feelings when you do."

"Okay," I smiled.

About the second week since my surrender, Jerry asked impatiently one evening, "Aren't you ever going to stop grinning?" I tried, I really did, and I couldn't help but smile.

I noticed, as I shopped or walked down the street, people I didn't know smiled at me. Why, I wondered? I remembered how my friends had once asked, "What's wrong, Marion? Life can't be that bad." Or they had said simply, "Smile."

One day I was pushing the boys in a cart at the grocery store and saw a lady with her children. I looked for several seconds, liking her happy attitude, before I realized it was *me* in the mirror. Then I knew. People were smiling at me because I was smiling at them!

I guess Jerry decided to try the acid test one night. We'd had an ugly feud going for years. It concerned my not keeping up with ironing his shirts. I would let them pile up, until he asked, "Going to iron this month, Marion?" I would snap back something smart. Once he went out and bought new shirts because I wouldn't iron.

We were matching a medical show. I was very interested in it. "Do I have a blue shirt for tomorrow?" he asked grimly.

Without a second thought I got up to look. When I found his shirts piled up on the ironing board, I started ironing. It never occurred to me to be angry. I was humming off-key as I ironed . . . "What a Friend We Have in Jesus."

Jerry stood in the door and looked around the room at the ironed shirts. I was ironing them all! He had watched me iron when I was in labor, or with the flu, or during an electrical storm, and he never had made a comment. But he came and put his arm around me now and said, "Let's see about getting you some help with the ironing, Mannie." I was deeply grateful, but kept ironing. "I don't really need anyone to iron. I just need to keep up with it. But thanks."

I stayed on a mountaintop for thirty-two days. One day I was talking with Christian friends about Jesus. They looked at me with disapproval and . . . disgust, it seemed to me. They criticized my new enthusiasm and the idea that Jesus cared about little things in our lives. Their remarks were subtle, but I felt them keenly. By the time I got home I knew what Bobby meant about not going on feelings. My feelings of peace and happiness and joy were fading. I felt separated from God. But I told myself, don't go on feelings; go on fact. You know God's in your life. Stop dwelling on their criticism. Pray they can come to total surrender, too. Love them. Jesus does.

I read my Bible for a while. Someone called and soon we were talking about God working in our lives, and I forgot about my friends' remarks.

I began letting the house go. There just didn't seem to be enough time in the day to clean and cook and read and talk about Jesus, too. One day Hilda gasped in horror as I opened a cabinet and dumped a sack of groceries inside and quickly shut the cabinet.

"How will you ever find anything? How can you stand that?" I laughed. It was a victory in my compulsively neat, orderly life.

Jerry had become used to a clean house and supper being ready when he came in from work. Now he'd come home to find the kitchen in a mess and no supper started. I'd be talking excitedly on the phone with a friend, and the children might be anywhere and into anything.

Jerry began to resent my talking on the phone, and he started to complain about the house. I had gone from one extreme to the other. He complained, too, that we didn't have to go to church everytime the doors opened. All I ever wanted to talk about were spiritual matters. Jerry listened for a while. When he tried to change the subject, I stubbornly refused. I shoved books, doctrines, and experiences at him until he almost ran from me.

At the Bible study I still attended, Tricia Jones began sharing that wives are not to teach their husbands. She also cautioned wives not to neglect their homes or families . . . and especially their husbands. "This is not God's plan," she told us. She really drove her point home. "Just shut up about spiritual matters until your husband asks you something."

Her timing was perfect for me. Friday morning when I got up I felt strongly impressed to give the house a thorough cleaning and cook a good supper. I decided to have a picnic with Jon and Jeremy under the weeping willow tree and listen to them. And I resolved not to talk on the phone at all.

"Guess what the Lord wants me to do today?" I called out to Jerry as he shaved. His eyes met mine in the mirror. I saw the dread in them. He probably thought I was going to preach somewhere.

I walked up to him and said apologetically, "God wants me to stay home all day and clean and cook and straighten out your sock drawer . . . and I'm not going to talk on the phone."

A quick smile appeared from behind the lather so that he looked like a happy clown. He gave me a quick kiss, and wiped the lather off my chin.

For a minute I was sure he was going to say, "Praise the Lord!" But he thought a moment and said instead, "Great."

21

I Like Me!

I couldn't have imagined the extent of the changes that would happen in me. After surrendering to Jesus *totally,* I hardly thought about myself. And I felt continually happy . . . a child-like happiness.

For many years I had thought about how I'd like to change myself. Five feet four inches instead of five feet seven. Naturally curly hair and flawless skin just like Snow White. And a turned-up nose. I visualized long fingernails and short feet, size 5½ B instead of 8½ AAA. And I wanted to be able to sing, to play the piano, and to speak in front of people . . . to enjoy being a hostess . . . never to scream at my children . . . and to be able to make decisions. My list of changes seemed unending.

I watched people, adding their attributes to my want list. In the summer I wanted a golden tan and blond hair. Even clothes became an obsession. I continually longed for a new outfit.

One day in Bible study Tricia said, "I want you to write down one thing about yourself that you don't like." We all laughed. I couldn't decide which thing to write down. There were so many. Finally I narrowed it down to either my nose or my head. My nose was too large, and my head was completely flat in the back. I wrote them both down. "Now thank God for those things you just wrote down," she laughed. "That's the way he made you."

I bowed my head, but I didn't pray. Not until that day in my den did I really give up wanting to be anything else except the way God made me. Then I was truly grateful for the way God had made me. Happiness, I decided, means accepting yourself. I no longer wanted to change.

I was still tone deaf, but I made a joyful noise without apology or embarrassment. I loved the words to the songs. My small artistic and writing talent suddenly seemed to grow like plants brought to the sunlight. I began to enjoy and to nurture these talents. I was confident God intended them for me and I wasn't nearly so hesitant about using them.

Having friends over became a joy. It had frightened me terribly at one time. I wanted everything just so. A dinner party for eight physically exhausted me. I couldn't enjoy my own parties. I labored over where each person would sit and imagined the conversations in advance.

What a wonderful discovery to invite eighty-five people for ice cream on the spur of the moment and enjoy the party, myself!

To control my screaming at my children was the hardest thing to let God change. Some days I did well, other days I had to continually confess my sin of impatience . . . and there were days that I would not admit I was wrong to scream at them.

Making decisions, however, turned into a simple feat . . . like catching on to the rules of a complicated game. Someone later explained to me: Once you make the most important decision in life—what are you going to do about Jesus?—other decisions become simple.

I knew that once I had worked myself into a severe gall bladder attack after five days of laboring over the question of where to put the punch bowl for a party. Going to the hospital was a way out—a very painful one—but a way out.

I knew what caused the attack but wouldn't admit it to myself, much less the young nurse who kept asking, "Has anything upset you?"

Grace Fields, who lived behind me, warned, "You can't stay this happy, Marion. You can't stay this happy and worry-free. You've been a worrier too long."

Grace was a retired schoolteacher. Although she had no children, my children (and my cat) adored her. Incredibly honest, she never said what she thought you wanted to hear, but she told it as she saw it. I was grateful for Grace's friendship. She marveled over a small violet nestled in green moss, and she loved books and cats as fiercely as I did. Our shyness or fear of rejection kept us apart when we first were neighbors, but we slowly grew to love one another.

I think I realized how much she meant to me when I would go to my kitchen window on days when I felt depression chasing me. I would look to see if her back door were open and if the sun were shining on her little back stoop. If it was, I breathed a little sigh of relief and eluded depression.

"It'll last, Grace. You'll see." That morning in her kitchen we read poems together, talked about Jesus, and prayed together.

The change in me was evident to myself and others. My hairdresser picked it up. She asked, "Have you got on new makeup?"

"No."

"Well, you've got something different. Whatever it is, I want some."

"It's Jesus. He's in control of my life."

"Really? Tell me about it."

I began sharing with her and gave her a "Four Spiritual Laws"

80

booklet. Sometimes as she did my hair she wanted to talk about Jesus. Other days she avoided the subject, and I remained silent.

One day while shopping I saw an acquaintance in my favorite dress shop. I stood at the door looking at her. She had a beautiful tan and small feet. Her nose turned up, too. She was telling the saleslady that she and her husband were going on a cruise . . . and they weren't taking the children. She carried three or four new outfits draped casually over her arm as she said, "We'll be gone about ten days."

I waited a moment for my reaction. No envy—not a bit. I didn't want to swap places with anyone. I wanted to run in and call out, "Have fun!"

22

Right Out of the Blue

It was three weeks since I'd prayed, "Thank you, anyway, Lord." Jerry and I hardly talked about the house. I began a program of rearranging the furniture and throwing away things to make more room.

Jerry and I shampooed the carpets, and I scrubbed walls. We had the outside of the house painted. I washed and ironed curtains joyfully, which was quite out of character for me. I stopped searching the want ads for a "large, comfortable, roomy house" for sale.

It was Friday. I had the good feeling that Friday often brings . . . cooking out, sleeping a bit late on Saturday, maybe putting out a new piece of shrubbery. Looking forward to Sunday and the services that day. And Friday was payday.

The telephone rang about 3:30. Jerry's secretary said, "Jerry said to tell you he'll be quite late. He just left for Atlanta."

"Thank you," I said, somewhat puzzled. He never left for Atlanta this late in the day. I couldn't imagine why he was going to Atlanta, but I was grateful for the call. I wouldn't be concerned about his being late.

When he came back I knew he had special news. I watched him eating, wondering about it. Finally he smiled at me. I noticed the blueness of his eyes. They often seemed to change color to indicate his moods. This true, sparkling blue meant "get ready for something fantastic!" I was ready.

Jerry's normally deep voice was softer than usual. "I went for an interview today. It's crazy how it happened. I just got this call late in the afternoon, and I went. It was just like something out of the blue."

"Yes," I grinned, "I guess it was."

"We won't know who got the job for sure until next week. Several people were interviewed."

"Oh, okay," I said.

I wasn't supposed to tell anyone but Hilda "guessed" the next day. "When will you know for sure? You can't move. You just can't."

"I'm not supposed to tell. Pretend you don't know."

"Okay. When will you know for sure?"

"I'm waiting for a call now. But you don't know that. I can't tell anyone yet." We sat in the shade of a large pine tree watching Jon and Jeremy playing, and I thought: Dear God, how can I leave here, how can I leave people and places I love so much?"

The phone rang, and Hilda and I both jumped up. "It's *my* phone, Hilda. You watch the boys," I laughed. I was back in thirty seconds. Hilda looked at me for a moment and said, "You're going." I nodded my head, feeling laughter and tears mixing together inside me.

Jerry told me that night that he thought we should list the house with a certain realty company. Since we would begin working in Atlanta right away, he planned to commute. I didn't protest, "But you'll get home so late." I wanted to do everything I could to help him.

The next day the real estate man came and evaluated the house. I was cleaning furiously and already had begun to pack a few things.

If I keep working, I won't think about leaving my friends. And I do want the house to look pretty for whoever God has for it.

I'm sure you have someone, Lord.

And he did. I knew as soon as I saw them coming up to the door, they were the right couple—the first people to look at it. Our house hadn't been for sale even thirty-six hours.

Young, appreciative, delighted, they oohed and ahhed, and I rejoiced silently. I liked them. I whispered to the real estate agent as they left, "They're going to buy it."

She whispered back, "You have a lot to learn about real estate. This is just the *first* couple." Then she glared at me impatiently.

But the next morning as we were praying about selling the house during our family devotional time, the doorbell rang. There stood our agent holding a contract with the most amazed look on her face. "Fastest house I've ever sold," she said in a monotone voice.

Jerry and I signed the contract, and in my heart I thanked and praised God. He'd been our agent.

23

My Song

Even though the house was sold I continued cleaning and scrubbing. I really enjoyed the hard work and the satisfaction of making it gleam. We planned to go to Atlanta the next week and look for a house. Friends warned us that it would be very difficult to find what we wanted—and the prices, we were told, were sky-high. One couple told us they rode 1,100 miles in a week looking for a house and didn't find anything they would even consider.

I just kept grinning, knowing our house was there. People laughed openly at my description of what I wanted when I mentioned the price we had agreed we could afford.

It was the Sunday before we were to go to Atlanta. It had been my Sunday to work in the nursery, but someone asked me to exchange days. The organist played softly as I went into the service to join Jerry and the girls.

The question came back. It had come for the last two Sundays during the invitation. *Will you respond publicly today? I've called you for three weeks now.*

But we settled this between you and me, Lord . . . in my den. I know it was real. . . I'm totally surrendered. Surely you don't want me to walk down that aisle again. It's not necessary.

Do you feel me calling you?

Yes, but I don't want to come.

I'm still calling you.

I know.

Are you coming today?

Let me think about it.

You've been thinking three weeks.

I'll think some more during the service.

You aren't going to have any peace until you do.

I know.

Then decide. Will you come today?

I don't want to.

I know that. Will you trust me and obey?

Is that why I'm sitting nearest the aisle where Jerry usually sits?

Will you come?

I'm almost sure I will.

Suppose I'd almost gone to the cross.

I'm going to listen to the sermon for a while.

My heart pounded so loudly I was certain people sitting around me heard it. I concentrated on what Dr. Griffith was saying.

"If we aren't willing to witness to people, to tell them about Jesus and what he's done for us personally . . . if we aren't willing to give ourselves to him completely, we are, in effect, still nailing his hands to the cross."

I'm calling you, Marion. Come publicly for total surrender. Privately isn't good enough. Will you come?

I want to.

Are you?

The first step will be so hard.

That's all you have to do. I'll do the rest, but you have to make that first move. Will you?

Yes . . . yes . . . yes! I'm coming. But . . .

What?

I need my song. You know how special it is to me . . . what the words mean to me. I need that melody and those words. That will make me feel your closeness. I know it will.

You can have your song.

A thought came plowing through my mind. *What? Are you some kind of a nut? These programs were printed a week ago. Do you actually believe just because you happen to want a special song, they have planned to sing it?*

Yes, I believe they will sing "Out of My Bondage" for me.

That's crazy. Childlike.

I need that song.

Well, you are foolish to think you can have it.

I think I like being foolish.

Look at the program. Check the hymn of invitation.

My hand reached for the program and stopped in midair. I could have continued reaching, but the thought not to look was so powerful, I replaced my hand in my lap.

Don't look. Trust me. I knew you would want that song.

Finally the service was over. We stood and the minister announced the hymn of invitation. I didn't hear him and wasn't sure of anything around me. It was just God and me there.

I stepped out on the first note. How easy going forward was! I walked down the aisle as the congregation sang, "Out of my bondage, sorrow, and night, Jesus, I come, Jesus, I come."

Others in the church were moving. A family I had been praying for came. Others were coming with decisions. I had to wait a moment to speak to Dr. Griffith. The singing continued and I listened, "Out of unrest and arrogant pride, Jesus I come, Jesus, I come."

The pastor took my hand and leaned forward to hear what I had to say. "This isn't a rededication. It's just all of me. Three weeks ago I surrendered myself totally to Jesus, and God wanted me to come forward today."

I walked back up the aisle with a calm, quiet joy that comes from obedience. As I slipped back into the pew, Jerry laid down the hymnbook and went forward.

I was singing now, "Out of myself to dwell in thy love, Out of despair to raptures above."

After church we went out to eat. I didn't order anything. I was so full of love and peace I didn't want to eat or talk. I just sat there feeling God's love and approval and wondering about the people eating all around me. How many of them had ever tasted the Bread of Life?

24

I Have a Testimony

Driving home from Tricia's Bible study with a friend, I suddenly slammed on the brakes. "I have a testimony," I announced to her, almost in disbelief. She smiled, "Of course you do. Every Christian does."

At the Bible study that morning several women had shared their testimonies. I could have listened to them all day. I sat nodding my head, understanding what they were saying. I knew of the searching . . . the knowledge that there must be more to life. And of finally finding it.

But Satan mocked me. "Ready to give your testimony, Marion? They'll ask you next. Ready to stand up in front of all those people and talk about Jesus? Surely you are. You're so excited about what he's done for you."

Speaking terrified me to a degree that was ridiculous. Any kind of speaking about anything. Describing how to make popsicles to a group would frighten me. Now I was sure I would be called to testify and fear began its work on me.

Then Satan suggested: "Back off, Marion. You still have time. Maybe this isn't as real as it seems. Cool it a bit. Move away from these people that are so excited about Jesus. You better!"

"I can't, I can't," I decided. "I won't move away . . . no matter what. It's real . . . what I've found."

God, I do have a testimony and I want to share it . . . I'm willing. But I can't talk in front of people . . . not yet, I don't see how, ever. But I'm not going to say I never will . . . I just don't see how I can. I love you, and I'm a new person, and I'm not moving away from you.

After I got home and fixed lunch for the boys, fear still followed me around like a chanting child—"You're scared. You're scared."

"God . . ." I just reached out for him, needing his comfort.

Can you continue to tell one person at a time about me?

You mean like I have been, over coffee at my kitchen table or on the phone?

Yes.

You mean that's witnessing?

Yes.

Then you have been using me!

I'll use anyone who's willing.

Tears of joy rolled down my face, "Me, Lord? You can use me!"

Certainly. Stop worrying about giving your testimony. Keep talking to people I'm sending your way.

I will. I will!

I worked at the hospital that week, and as I came through the cafeteria line I didn't see anyone I knew to eat with. As I paid for my food, I saw a lady eating alone. My heart pounded as I got the message right away. *Eat with her and tell her about me.*

A stranger? Not a stranger, Lord. I can't.

I stood frozen by the cashier, who gave me an odd look. I wanted to run out and forget my food, but instead I walked over toward the lady who was eating alone. She looked up and smiled. I hesitated, then managed, "Are you eating alone?"

"Yes."

"Do you want some company?"

"Yes, I hate to eat alone. Please join me."

In a few minutes we were chatting like old friends. She didn't have children and wanted to talk about mine. She laughed at stories about the twins—"My, you should write a book."

"I am."

"You are?"

"Yes."

I thought back a moment to when I'd first toyed with the idea of writing my testimony. The thought had been as tiny as a rain drop, and I laughed at it and mentally thumped it away. But I began jotting down experiences and recorded others in my mind. I'd almost completely given up ever writing anything. Almost. A few friends had encouraged me, and I thought: Well, I can write it down for me and my family and a few close friends. I can do that." I had no idea how to write a book, but my notes began to grow and somewhere along the way I realized it could turn into a book. Maybe it would live in the old secretary where I kept things I didn't want to lose.

But I was writing it. I just didn't know what to do with it.

"What's your book about?"

"The children and how hard motherhood is . . . things like that."

"I mean the main idea. What is it you want to say?"

I looked at her and said, "I have recently totally given up—surrendered my life to Jesus. He's in control now. It's so wonderful I want to share it with others."

She stopped her fork in midair, then replaced it on her plate still full of food. "How did you do it? I'm a Sunday School teacher, and I have been trying for twenty years to do what you've done. Tell me about it."

Our food forgotten, we talked, and I answered her questions as best I could. Then it was time to pick up the boys at nursery school. I had to go.

But will she surrender to you, Lord?

That's not your worry. You did what I asked.

25

Dear Marion . . .

I continued to work on my book. I hid it as I wrote. Only Julie read it. She would come in from school and ask, "Got any more? Let me read it." The book was just one long paragraph then. In terrible shape. But I didn't know that. Julie would flop her books down and read, and I would leave the room.

Often she would find me and hand it back to me with tears in her eyes. "It's good, Mama. Keep writing."

I would cry over her encouragement and continue writing sentences a page long, no chapters or paragraphs.

I couldn't remember when I didn't like to write. A stack of white paper fascinated me. I had to put something on it. Many days as a child I waited upstairs in the director's room of the Granite City Bank for my mother to finish work. There was always a stack of paper on the long shiny table. I looked down on a one-way street at the people and watched them. Then I took some of the white paper and wrote or drew what I saw. Time flew by.

In college, my English professor, Dr. George Walker, handed my first theme back with an A plus at the top. Then scrawled in an almost illegible handwriting was, "You can write. Learn to spell." He had circled thirteen misspelled words. All that day I said the phrase to myself, "You can write." I never missed one of Dr. Walker's classes. I often imagined what it would be like to be studying journalism. I hadn't mentioned to my mother that desire when she suggested a business course. I knew it was difficult for her to send me to college. A business course could always be used . . . writing couldn't. Only the best writers could make a living at it.

After I was married I submitted articles to magazines. My first rejection slip crushed me. In fact, I only slid it halfway out of the envelope, then quickly put it back, not even reading it. I stuffed it with the returned article into a drawer. I vowed never to submit anything again. But I did and I got used to the rejection slips.

One week before I "gave up" in my den, I rose early to read before the children were up. Words jumped out at me. "God wants you to thank him for bad things." I shut the book and pondered this idea. I told God I would thank him for the next bad thing that happened to me, and at my house I wouldn't have to wait very long, I knew!

Just after lunch I opened the dishwasher to discover it was full of water. In my mind I could hear Jerry fussing because I hadn't scraped the plates properly. Then I remembered, and I prayed, "Thank you, Lord, for this broken dishwasher." Through a series of events that wouldn't seem too unusual if I hadn't been sure God was using that prayer to teach me, I managed to fix the dishwasher. I sat down at my typewriter in the kitchen and wrote about it, finishing the story in about five minutes. I called it, "Thank You, Lord, for My Broken Dishwasher." A *Guideposts* magazine was lying beside the typewriter. I found the address and sent the article to them. I was still so excited about God working in my life that the article was almost an afterthought.

For years I had imagined what it would be like to go to the mailbox and find a letter of acceptance. I had lived it mentally hundreds of times.

One Saturday morning there was an envelope with a return address marked *Guideposts*. It wasn't thick enough to contain my manuscript. I tore it open and could read only the first line. "We are accepting for publication your article . . ." I couldn't read the rest for tears.

I jumped up and down and screamed, just like I had imagined. Then I ran for the house. Both our families were visiting us, and they thought something had happened to one of the children. I couldn't make them understand. I just kept screaming and crying and jumping up and down. The children appeared, one by one, and stared at me in silent wonder. Mother was pitching one of *their* fits. Then I noticed something else in the envelope. It was a check for fifty dollars. I had no idea they would pay me. When no one was around I whispered the word *accepted* to myself.

My family rejoiced with me. Jerry grinned silently. He had never understood this thing I had about writing. Later I spit on the signature of the letter just to see it smear. It was real! I'd received so many form letters. Then I read the name I'd smeared. Dina Donohue had written me a warm, personal letter, and I felt she was a Christian, excited about Jesus.

Immediately, I thought again of the book I was writing.

Bobby took me seriously when I talked about writing a book. She said confidently, "You'll write it . . . and it'll be published." She said it the same way she had said, "The Holy Spirit sent you."

One day I felt I had to have some concrete encouragement to continue seriously writing the book. Who could I get encouragement from? I didn't know anyone in the publishing world.

How about Dina Donohue? She's written you four letters concerning your article. You could write to her.

I can't. Oh, I can't. What would she think? So I want to have a book published, so what? I've had one article accepted, and here I go telling Mrs. Donohue I want to write a book.

Three days later I did write to her, but decided I wouldn't mail it. Maybe just writing would make me feel better. As I finished, I heard the squeak of the mail truck's brakes. I stuck on a stamp and ran to put the letter in the box.

Well, I did it. But what am I trying to find out? I wrote her a three-page letter about wanting to write a book. Big deal.

Would you like some encouragement . . . or even discouragement?

Oh yes.

What does she call you when she writes to you?

Mrs. West.

Suppose she wrote, "Dear Marion . . ."

Oh, yes. I would take that as a sign from you that I must continue . . . even though I don't know how to write a book or how to get one published.

In less than a week a letter came from *Guideposts*. It was marked D. Donohue in the corner. I opened it and read, "Dear Marion, I can no longer call you Mrs. West, for I feel I know you far too well . . ."

I ran to the typewriter, found my notes, and began writing again. *Out Of My Bondage* was getting thicker . . . if not better.

91

26

House Hunting

The real estate company in Athens that sold our house had recommended another company in Atlanta to work with us. I answered the phone one evening to hear: "Hi, Mrs. West. I'm Betty Westbrook. We're going to find a home for you."

I liked her voice—it was full of enthusiasm. I wondered if she were a Christian. We talked for nearly twenty minutes, and Jerry and I planned to come to Atlanta the next weekend and look for our house. She said she could show homes any day except Sunday. "I'll be in church on Sunday." I liked that.

Jerry's parents came to keep the children, and we left early Saturday morning. I'd never seen such rain. It was so thick it looked like a fog. As we dressed that morning we realized neither of us had cashed a check. "Now where can we get a check for over a hundred dollars cashed at 7 A.M.?" Jerry asked.

"The Golden Pantry," I answered.

"You know they don't cash checks for over ten dollars."

"If Jim is there he will cash it for us." Jim Copeland, the manager, had worked in the bank with my mother when I was a child. I saw him often then. Now we often talked about old times when I ran in for a loaf of bread or ice cream for the children. "How's your mother," he'd always ask.

"He won't do it," Jerry insisted. But I was already running out the door.

Please let Jim be working this morning, Lord.

"What can I do for you so early?" Jim smiled at me.

"I need money . . . lots of money."

"Is this a holdup?" he grinned.

"Any chance you could cash a check for $135?" He opened the cash register and said, "You can have all I've got." Then he counted out the money. "Want some more? Got plenty."

"No . . . this is just great. Thanks." I told him why I needed it.

His smile vanished. "You've got a rough day ahead. I used to live in Atlanta. Finding a house is tough." He looked out the window at the nasty weather. "This rain won't help. I'm going to say a prayer for you today."

"Thanks, Jim, for the money and the prayer."

I was excited about driving to Atlanta with Jerry. Alone, we could talk without interruption, or just be quiet together.

As we sat in the carport with the rain beating down outside, we asked God to watch over our children, give us a safe trip, and lead us to our house.

As we drove, the rain became worse, so that Jerry drove slowly. "Thank you, Lord, for this rain," I prayed silently. "I don't understand it, but someone must need it. Maybe you want to show us a leaky basement. But if it's all right with you, we would love to see some sunshine."

Jerry said something I'll always remember because it's not the kind of thing he usually says . . . but it was the kind of thing I loved.

"Underneath this rain the sun is shining."

"Right," I agreed, but I knew what he was saying, and I loved him for it.

We found Walter Scott Realty and waited for Betty Westbrook. I became impatient and thought: She's probably forgotten you. Doesn't have a thing lined up. Just then a small, red-haired, laughing-eyed woman appeared, out of breath. A few drops of rain remained in her hair. "I'm sorry I'm late. The rain held me up."

In her office we talked about the house we wanted. *But is she a Christian, Lord?*

Betty was telling a story, "Someone asked me if I was satisfied with my religion. I said religion isn't so important . . . I'm satisfied with my Lord." She radiated when she said it.

She is! Thank you, Lord.

At that moment the sun came out. Brilliant, it flooded the office so that I squinted my eyes for a moment.

We went outside to begin our search. A breeze rapidly blew away the clouds. We watched them disappear. As we got into her car the sky was a brilliant blue.

We looked at houses all day. I lost track of the number. We stopped long enough to eat lunch. Betty and I talked incessantly. Jerry smiled a lot and joined in when he could.

We were amazed at the price of houses . . . and we couldn't seem to find our house. We needed lots of room and a large lot, and a not-so-large price. One house we couldn't see because a child had lost the key. Betty seemed annoyed, but smiled quickly, "Well, folks, we'll just have to say 'Thank you, Lord,' for the lost key." Betty was becoming dearer all the time.

We hadn't found our house, but I still knew it was there.

Betty said she would like to show us the house that we hadn't seen if she could locate the key. Maybe we could see it Sunday after church.

I was so tired I ached all over. When I slept, I dreamed of our house with the playroom. Instead of going to church as we had planned, we went to see a friend in the hospital. It was a painful visit. She had incurable cancer.

We met Betty and went to see the house. She had found the key. Just before we got there Betty said, "Know what? This is one of the houses whose ads you clipped out of the Atlanta paper and sent to me."

"Really . . . well, maybe this is it." As we stood on the front porch, I looked through a window and felt a shiver. "This is it," I said.

We went in. There was the avocado carpeting, the slate foyer entrance, the largest kitchen I'd ever seen, with avocado cabinets. The den was tremendous . . . like two dens, nearly. Betty and I were squealing like teenagers at a ball game.

Beyond the den was a hall . . . and at the end of the hall . . . the playroom! With red carpet, paneled walls, and three low windows. I looked at it through tears. I wanted to throw my arms around the whole room and say "I love you."

Upstairs were four bedrooms with avocado carpeting. I like avocado! One of the three bathrooms was papered in a pattern I had wanted to use to repaper our bathroom in Athens. The backyard was large and fenced in, with trees for the boys to climb and a little shed they could play in.

I was afraid to ask the price. I didn't have to. Betty was quoting it, almost as if she didn't believe it. It was five hundred dollars under what we had agreed we could pay for a house!

27

Give It Up

Our house was getting more and more empty as I packed things. Some items I didn't want the movers to handle. The children seemed to accept our moving well. None of the sadness crept back into my heart. I just looked ahead joyously, trusting that no sadness would come.

Several of our friends gave going-away parties for us. I looked forward to moving into our new home. I showed the children and friends the pictures of it, and I looked at them every day.

Betty called often about small details of the contract. Sometimes she called me just to share what God was doing in our lives. I loved talking with her.

One Sunday night she called. "Marion, get Jerry on the other phone. I have to talk to both of you."

"Okay," I said. "Go ahead. We're both here." *Something is wrong. Her voice doesn't sound right.*

"I've got bad news, folks. The owners of the house are backing out of selling. You are legally right, but it can get nasty and involved if we try to move a man out of his home when he doesn't want to move. But don't give up. We've got to have faith."

I felt like the breath had been knocked out of me . . . and sick at my stomach. Jerry asked questions about the legal recourse we had. His voice was calm and earnest. I didn't say anything. One word would have reduced me to tears. I didn't know how to pray about it. I didn't feel like praying. I wanted to stomp and scream and yell, "It's ours. The contract is signed."

Jerry went to Atlanta Monday to look for another house with Betty. I didn't go. I couldn't give up my dream house. Jerry and Betty were unable to find anything else. When I told some of my friends what had happened, a few of them smiled and said, "God is testing you."

I didn't like the test, and I didn't care much whether I passed or not. I just wanted my house. I moped around a couple of days, feeling sick and almost frightened.

Enough of this, I decided. I picked up my Bible my mother had given me when I accepted Christ and joined the church. I read the inscription, "May this book ever guide you through life. Lovingly, Mother. 1944."

Guide me now. I need guidance. Please God, give me something. He gave me Psalm 57. When I finished reading it, I called my mother long distance at the bank to tell her joyfully, "I've given up the house. Don't try to understand. Just be happy with me. I've really done it. Read Psalm 57 when you get home."

I told my friends what I'd been able to do.

"Where will we live?" Julie and Jennifer asked as they looked sadly at the pictures of what was to have been our house. "God has us a house. You'll see. Don't worry."

Two friends arranged a good-bye coffee for me. Some of them understood and rejoiced over my calmness. Others said, "You must be crazy. Why aren't you in Atlanta right now looking for a house?"

I was able to smile at either reaction. God knew we had to move in nine days. He could do anything in nine days. He created the world in only seven.

There I was—me—the worrying champion, unable to worry!

Right after Betty first gave us the bad news I had written the owners. My letter explained that we felt God had led us to that house; we weren't being stubborn . . . we just loved it and wanted it. We were praying that they might have a change of heart. As I mailed my letter to them, they mailed us a letter, also. It was written by a lawyer to inform us officially that the house was no longer available. It was very impressive-looking and registered. As I signed for it, I remembered how simple mine was in appearance and content.

A meeting was set up six days before we had to be out of our house in Athens. Jerry and representatives from the real estate company and the owners would meet in Atlanta to try and reach an agreement.

They were to meet on a Tuesday at two in the afternoon. Jennifer and Julie prayed in school. Many of my friends agreed to pray on that day. I knew Tricia, Bobby, Frances, Joan, Hilda, and others were praying. The request had been placed in a prayer channel in Athens; Christians I didn't even know were also praying. I prayed as I went about my morning household duties. "Lord, if that house is for us, change the owner's mind. We want it only on friendly terms. We don't want to fight for it. I want Jerry and the owners to agree and shake hands before they walk out of that meeting. If the house is not for us, give us another one.

I shopped for groceries. But I didn't stop praying. I was putting items in the cart when I saw Hilda. "Are you praying?"

"Yes," she assured me. Others called to tell me they were praying throughout the day.

At two I got on my knees by my bed. "Lord, have I forgotten to pray about anything? Please remind me."

If Jerry gets angry, it will show in his eyes and voice, no matter what he is saying. Yes, oh, yes. "Lord, give Jerry a gentle, calm voice filled with patience and understanding. Let his eyes shine a clear blue, like they do when he is the happiest."

Until three I continued praying as I worked. It had been a day of prayer that had brought me unspeakable peace. "Thank you. Whatever has happened, thank you. I know you were at that meeting."

The phone started to ring again. Friends wanted to know if Jerry was home yet and what had happened. I didn't pace the floor or look out the window for Jerry. When I heard his car I just felt happiness. Whatever he had to tell me, I had already accepted. He came in the back door . . . and I knew. No words were necessary.

97

The sparkling blue eyes said it all.

But Jerry, a man of few words said, "We got it. It's ours."

Oh, Lord, how good you are! How wonderful you are! How marvelous are your ways!

28

Spiritual Novocain

Bobby Leverett told me she wanted to see me a few moments before we left. She said she would come by my house.

Don't let her say good-bye, Lord.

She followed me, and together we went into my empty house. Our steps echoed as we walked through the den. Movers were taking out the beds. "I want to pray with you," she said softly.

We looked at each other and smiled . . . thinking the same Scripture about praying in the closet, I suppose. We went into my bedroom closet and with the movers talking loudly on the outside of the closet, we prayed in the privacy of the empty closet. We prayed about a decision Bobby and her family were about to make and for us as we moved . . . especially that I not get lost driving. Bobby didn't have a sense of direction, either, and understood my fear of getting lost.

Then she handed me a gift. "Open it," she smiled. I could hardly believe what she had given me. Only last Sunday I had stood looking through a window at it. The store wasn't open. I wanted it so much I thought of going back on Monday and buying it for myself . . . except that it was the kind of thing someone gives you. I wanted someone to give it to me.

"I'll hold it in my lap all the way." I smiled down at the Holly Hobbie plate. The picture depicted a very determined little girl who held a picnic basket as she climbed over a fence. The words said: "To the house of a friend . . . the way is never long."

Bobby turned quickly and walked out. Her steps echoed while

I kept my gaze on the little girl on the plate.

Frances had earlier brought me an African violet. These two gifts I would take in the car with me.

I suddenly remembered that Jeremy and Jon had a dental appointment. Hilda took them for me as I watched the men putting the last few items on the truck.

Grace Fields was going to feed our temperamental cat, Wingate, until we moved into our house. I was grateful that Grace loved cats like I did. She wouldn't just plop the food down. She would talk to our cat, calling her by name and stroking her gently. Grace wouldn't come over to say good-bye, I knew that. Maybe she'd stand on her little back stoop in the sunshine and wave. *Let this spiritual novocain last, Lord. Don't let it wear off now.*

Jerry and I were mopping and vacuuming when Hilda brought the boys back. "They're fine. No cavities," she said. "Thanks, Hilda." We were talking like the circumstances were normal . . . like all the furniture was in the house, and she had just run over for a moment.

Then it was time to go. I felt butterflies in my stomach. I had to drive our car while Jerry drove a borrowed truck with many of our items in it. I was nervous about driving to Atlanta. I couldn't read a map and without any sense of direction, I knew if I lost sight of Jerry, I'd be in a real mess. Friends of mine drove to Florida and even up north alone, but I was scared driving to Atlanta from Athens, about 50 miles. Julie and Jeremy would ride with me. Julie had a good sense of direction and would remain cool if we did become lost. Jeremy wouldn't care if we became separated from the others— he liked adventure.

Jennifer, who was as terrified of becoming lost as I was, and Jon, who liked to stick close to his daddy in any situation, would ride with Jerry. And I got the dog, Muff.

We all climbed into the car and truck. I looked out the car window. Our cat sat dozing under her favorite bush. Grace came out her back door. She stood there watching us. I saw she had cat food in her hand and knew she would feed Wingate and talk to her before we were out of the city limits. *Thank you, Lord, that Grace will love Wingate.*

99

Neighbors were coming out now and waving from their yards. No one *said* good-bye. Julie and Jennifer cried. Their little friends cried, too. The boys were excited. For some reason they thought going to Atlanta meant living at Six Flags. The dog was already asleep under my feet, relieved that she wasn't being left with the cat.

Jerry came over to the car to give me more instructions about following him. He knew I was frightened, but we didn't talk about it. He looked over his shoulder and said: "Well, house, you won't have to stay alone even one night. Your new owners will be here in about two hours."

That comment from him made me feel so good I almost forgot about being afraid of driving to Atlanta.

Jerry cranked up the truck and motioned me in a teasing manner to follow. I cranked the car and pressed down on the gas. The spiritual novocaine wasn't going to wear off. I was going to be fine. I waved to Grace, Hilda, Chris, Paula, and Mary.

I didn't look back.

29

Atlanta

We stopped for something to eat near Atlanta, and Jerry told me I was following him so closely that I was going to drive into the back of the truck. He didn't tell me that we would hit the five o'clock traffic in Atlanta and have to drive to the other side of the city and then get on the notorious South Expressway.

As we drove on, I didn't look to the left or right. I just kept my eyes on the tag of Jerry's truck, and I prayed. Julie prayed, too.

I stayed close to Jerry going around Atlanta on the expressway. Then we came to a bottleneck situation. Traffic was bumper to bumper. When I saw what I had to do, tears brimmed my eyes.

To get onto the expressway, I must pull out in front of whizzing cars that couldn't stop to let me in. I felt sick. Jerry inched his way toward the exit. Then he pulled into a small space between cars that I never would have attempted. If I didn't follow instantly, we'd be separated. Julie watched me. *Lord, stop somebody, please.*

"Go, Mama," Julie shouted. A man was letting me in. We all waved to him like politicians in a parade. Jerry was only three cars up, and I knew I'd get behind him again soon.

The traffic was unbelievable. The fact that I was driving in it was even more unbelievable. I remembered what several friends had told me, "I'm going to pray until I know you are there safely." I was grateful for their prayers now.

Soon Jerry was in front of me again, and Jennifer waved joyfully as if we had been separated in space. Jerry was laughing and looking at me in his rearview mirror with approval, too.

Finally he signaled to turn. *Wonderful. We'll be off this expressway soon. And I won't drive anywhere, Lord. I'll just stay at the apartment.* Then I saw the sign, the same one I'd seen in the want ads. Arrowhead Village. *Oh, thank you, Lord. We made it.*

It was unbearably hot . . . and not a tree in sight. The dog panted and drooled on me, anxious to get out of the car. Jeremy cried for some water. Julie looked relieved that we were here safely, and we all waited for Jerry to get the key to our apartment.

I hope my furniture is all right, Lord. Let it be stored safely. Thank you for this apartment. And thank you for the house that we'll be moving into soon.

30

Moving Day Again

The apartment was a novelty for the children. They loved the pool and tennis courts. The dog hated it and followed me constantly, shaking and nervous . . . probably longing for green grass and trees.

I was with Muff. . . yearning for trees and a yard of our own.

On the third day rain set in, and it rained for three days. Jerry drove our only car to work. The children, Muff, and I sat on our miniature front porch watching the rain and getting slightly wet. Inside, the boys were without toys or games. They amused themselves by tumbling down the winding stairs in the packing boxes.

The morning of the fourth day of rain I awoke and prayed, "Lord, I need to see an adult. I'm lonely and getting short with the children." About ten that morning, Gayle Carter, a friend who had been a neighbor when we both lived in Macon called. She now lived in Atlanta and wanted to take us all to an antique place to browse. "Oh, thank you, Lord. What a difference her call makes."

The sun came out that afternoon, and my loneliness disappeared.

Our first Sunday in Atlanta we went to First Baptist Church on Peachtree Street. After church we planned to drive out to let the children see the house and to measure the doors in the boy's room. I had begged Jerry into letting me bring their closet doors with the mural painted on them. He agreed, and we had them in the truck.

The girls were horrified to find that we were going to church in downtown Atlanta all piled in the front of a truck. Jerry wasn't too wild about the idea, but the boys and I thought it was great. I love trucks . . . any kind of truck. Hilda was the only friend I had who loved trucks, too. She would have enjoyed going to church in the truck with us.

It was Father's Day and Dr. Charles Stanley preached a sermon that I loved. Still, I looked forward to finding *our* church. We liked this one, but it was too far from where we would be living.

The children loved the house and yard and could hardly wait to move in. Later in the week, Jerry said the owners had decided that they could move out earlier than we had agreed on and that we could move in in *two* weeks.

Our moving date was set again, and we took the children to Elberton, 100 miles away. The movers agreed to bring our furniture out of storage and move us on the short notice we'd given them. I had all the utilities put in our name, cleaned out the refrigerator, and packed once again to move. We had been in the apartment only three weeks, instead of the anticipated three months!

In the morning, I thought, we'll really move into our house—finally. The phone interrupted my happy thoughts. Jerry answered it, and I could tell immediately from his eyes something was wrong. He hung up the phone with defeat. "They aren't going to let us move. I only had his word that we could move this weekend, and now he says we can't."

I sort of exploded. Jerry's calmness made me even angrier. I cried and talked myself into exhaustion. Finally, I slept fitfully, waking several times to pray, "No, Lord, I can't say thank you. I'm too tired and disappointed."

Jerry went to work in the morning, and I was left alone wondering when we would go to Elberton to get the children and again set up housekeeping. I read my Bible a while, and then I prayed: "Thank you. I don't understand it; I'm angry. It's hard to trust, but I want to. Help me trust. Give me the peace that I know is possible." Betty Westbrook called and said not to give up. She believed that we still might move the next day.

"No way, Betty. We've canceled the movers."

"I'm still praying, Marion. I'm still believing." The operator interrupted our conversation. "I have an emergency call from Mr. Jerry West."

"Call me," Betty insisted before we hung up.

I hung up praying, "Not the children, Lord. Please."

The phone rang loudly, and I picked it up instantly.

"Mannie . . ."

Oh, Lord, I know from his voice. Thank you!

"What is it, Jerry?" I asked anyway.

"We're moving tomorrow. The movers can still swing it. I'm picking up the key to the house tonight. I'll be a little late, but I'll have the key when I get there."

"Jerry . . ." I blubbered, crying loudly.

"I thought you'd be happy . . ." he began.

"I've never been so happy."

Tomorrow Lord . . . we'll be in our house . . . finally, thank you.

31

Our Church

The children and our parents arrived the next day, and Julie and Jennifer squealed with delight over their separate rooms. Jon and Jeremy ran outside and immediately climbed a tree and happily sat in it.

I was overjoyed that Big could come with them. He moved slowly, and each step was painful. He was a bit confused about where he was . . . but the smiling children and all of us around him seemed to indicate to him that wherever it was, it was just fine. Slowly he made his way through each room, carefully looking overhead at the ceiling and the walls and the flooring. Then he went out the back door ever so slowly and found a shady spot under a tree. He announced he would sit there until they were ready to go. I thought as I looked at him, "You aren't going to be able to make this trip many more times." I had no idea that was the only time he would make it.

We moved in on a Friday. Sunday morning we visited a nearby church. We decided that we must find a church that each one of us felt was right. That's how we would know where we belonged . . . each of us would want to stay there. And we prayed, asking God to lead us to the right church.

The next Sunday a neighbor invited us to her church. The regular pastor wasn't preaching. I had heard of the guest minister, Clifton Fite. I knew he had written a book about his son, David, who had been imprisoned by Castro. Reverend and Mrs. Fite had gone to Cuba and prayerfully and determinedly obtained their son's release.

Mr. Fite preached a simple sermon about salvation; and I quickly wiped away my tears. His church was across town . . . too far for us to attend, but I would never forget him or the message I heard that day.

The next Sunday we returned to Mountain Park First Baptist Church in Stone Mountain. Again, a guest was in the pulpit. A layman, Lynwood Maddox, shared his testimony. Jerry and I liked his simple message.

The pastor of the church, Dr. Gerald Bagwell, came to see us during the week. About twelve others came by. We learned that Mountain Park had a bus ministry and an active outreach program. I loved this idea . . . of reaching out to people. This church really seemed to care about people . . . all people.

At the close of Lynwood Maddox's testimony, we stood to sing the hymn of invitation. Our family looked at each other a moment. Then we were all making our way to the aisle. It felt right to be declaring our intention to become part of Mountain Park's fellowship.

The hymn of invitation was "Out of My Bondage"!

Right away I was asked to take several jobs in the church. The church was growing rapidly, and they needed help in many areas. I remembered some of the jobs I had taken at Beech Haven in Athens. I took them to satisfy people. I knew that now. I had promised God I wouldn't do that again. It was a hard promise to keep. Committees and individuals asked me to take a teaching job. But I didn't get a go-ahead from God. Instead I heard: *Wait, trust me.* What would people think about my not taking a job? *Please, Lord, give me a go-ahead. I'm feeling uncomfortable saying no so much.*

There was no answer. "I'll wait, Lord," I finally prayed. "You tell me what and when." That was a difficult prayer for me. I hated waiting for anything.

Dr. Bagwell saw me in the parking lot one day. We began talking. Soon we were talking about Jesus. I liked that. Ministers often spoke about Jesus in the pulpit . . . but talking about him in the parking lot made me feel closer to my new minister. We talked about the second coming of Jesus and some sermons he was preparing about it. Then he said: "Hey, I hear you do posters. Will you make us one? The Fites are joining us. Mr. Fite will be our associate pastor in charge of outreach."

"Really," I squealed. "Oh, how wonderful. I love Mr. Fite."

"You'll love Mrs. Fite, too. I'm grateful God is sending them to us. Make us a poster welcoming them. They'll be here next Sunday."

That was my first job for my new church, and I accepted it joyfully.

105

I prayed about the poster and I added: "Lord, I love making posters. Let me do more."

The Fites were presented to the church the next week and as I went through the line and introduced myself, Mrs. Fite held my hand tightly. "You made that beautiful poster, didn't you? Thank you. That's just how we got here."

Her genuine appreciation warmed me. I went back to look at it again. It was a black silhouette of a large hand reaching down to a church and congregation. Two people were stepping out of the hand. A small child was running toward them with a single flower. The poster read, "Thank you, Lord, for the Fites."

We were meeting many people in the church, but I still didn't have names and faces together. In church service one day I prayed, "Lord, I need a spiritual sister . . . someone I can pray and share with."

I have one for you. I looked around for my "sister." I started with the choir. My eyes went up one row and down another . . . they stopped . . . how had I missed her before? What a joy and radiance she had as she sang about Jesus—and she looked like someone I knew. Who was it?

Well, never mind, I intend to get to know her. After church I made my way to her. "You sing about Jesus like you really know him and love him."

"I do . . . he's changed me. He's the greatest thing that's ever happened to me."

"Let's get together and talk about him. I want to know how you met him."

"When?" she asked immediately.

"In the morning . . . nine, at my house."

"Fine. Where do you live?"

As I told her, she interrupted, "I know where that is. I'll be there."

She started to walk away, and so did I. Suddenly we both walked back toward each other smiling. "What's your name?" I laughed.

"Venera Weldon. What's yours?"

"Marion West."

"See you in the morning, Marion," she smiled.

Venera came right at nine, and we sat in my kitchen drinking coffee and talking about how we came to know Jesus personally.

She had been a Christian nine years. Back then someone "twisted her arm," and she attended a revival because she couldn't get out of it. During the invitation her oldest child, Donnie, went forward with a friend. She was moved to go also and accepted Christ as her Savior. "I had no idea what I'd turned away from all my life. I didn't know God loved me just as I was and was waiting for me to respond."

As Venera talked I slowly realized who she looked like. Anne Litaker! My neighbor in Athens who'd given me ten dollars worth of change. I thought that her heart must be a lot like Anne's, too.

I joined the Sunday School class that Venera taught. I had visited several others, but felt I belonged in hers. She said one day that she needed a class secretary and an outreach chairman. The thought of keeping any kind of records was repulsive to me . . . but the outreach chairman . . . I liked the sound of it, even though I wasn't sure exactly what it meant.

I wonder if I could do that, Lord. I think I would like to. Let her ask me if you want me to do it.

"And for our outreach chairman, I'd like to ask Marion West," Venera smiled directly at me.

"Yes, yes," I grinned. I was excited about my second job in the church. And I was staying busy making posters. I was amazed that so many people couldn't make them and were delighted to have me make their posters.

As outreach chairman I contacted members who were absent and visited newcomers. It was the one-to-one relation that I loved and felt comfortable with.

Two weeks after I'd accepted the job, Venera told me that I was to preside over the class each morning and have the opening prayer and make announcements.

Lord, I wouldn't have taken it if I'd known that!

That's why you didn't know. You can do it. And Venera would become a friend with whom I could share both sorrow and joy.

32

A Small Table

Our first Christmas in our new home was both festive and sad. My stepfather, Big, had been returned to the hospital from a nursing home. Mother wouldn't leave him, so Jerry's folks came over on Christmas Day without them. It was the first time all of our families hadn't spent Christmas Day together and the first time in my life I wasn't with my mother on Christmas Day.

We did drive to Elberton two days before Christmas and surprised Mother. And we visited Big in the hospital and gave him his gifts. We took a small, artificial tree already decorated, complete with tiny lights, to his room. He smiled at it and opened the gifts we took him. We took him to the chapel to open the gifts so the children could see him. He laughed a lot, but tired easily. The little tree seemed to brighten up his room, and he realized it was Christmas. It was the same tree we had taken once to Coy's room.

Despite Big's illness, Mother was still working—in fact she hadn't missed a day's work at the bank where she had been employed nearly thirty-eight years. I had watched her enter his hospital room many times. She always wore a smile for him.

I thought about her devotion to Big as we drove back to Atlanta. At home, we found a lot of Christmas cards in our mail box. I stood at my kitchen table reading them. I still wore my coat. An unfamiliar handwriting caught my attention. I liked surprise cards, especially at Christmas. The card was from Bill, the boy who had needed someone to care. He wrote: "I have found myself in God's world. I plan to enter a Christian vocation and pattern my life after that of Jesus Christ. God bless you all."

It had been over two years since we had met in the emergency room.

Oh, thank you, Lord. Thank you for what Bill has found, and thank you that he wrote me about it. Stay close to him now.

I answered the doorbell with tears streaming down my face, and

Venera looked surprised. "Happy tears," I managed and handed her the card. I had told her about Bill. She smiled at me quickly and with understanding.

After Christmas I thought about my writing again. *Lord, if I had a place to write, I might write more. I just don't have anywhere to write. I need a little table.*

Have you looked for one?

I really haven't, and I guess you expect me to do that. If I find one at Ruth's for twenty-five dollars, I'll get it.

Ruth's shop was my favorite antique place. She drove a hard bargain but had lovely items, as well as junk. We were going to see Big in Elberton, and I mentally planned to stop by Ruth's. The table I envisioned was odd-shaped . . . not very wide, oblong . . . to fit into a small space between the kitchen stove and the back door.

Jerry agreed to stop by Ruth's with me. I saw the table right away and tried not to keep looking at it longingly. Finally, I asked, "How much is that little, old table, Ruth?"

"Thirty dollars," She didn't bat an eye.

Okay, Lord. I tried. "I only have twenty-five dollars, Ruth."

"It's worth more than thirty," she said.

"Sorry . . . I like it, but twenty-five is all I can pay." I walked away.

"All right. You're one of my favorite people. Twenty-five."

"If it doesn't fit, I'll have to return it, okay?"

"Okay," she sighed.

It fit perfectly, and I began writing. I wrote while I cooked. I continued sending articles to *Guideposts*. They were returned, but with lovely, encouraging letters from Dina Donohue. I had a file of letters from her, but except for that one time, she still called me Mrs. West.

Guideposts sponsored a contest. The prizes were trips to New York for a week's intensive study in religious writing. I decided to enter, in spite of my great fear of flying and not knowing what I could work out about caring for the children if I won. I wanted to write about Bill and our encounter in the emergency room.

109

I began thinking about a desk, a real desk, like my mother used to have at the bank. When I was a little girl I would sit in her chair sometimes and pull out the drawers and touch the smoothness of the wood. Maybe someday I'd have a desk like that.

It was someday. I needed my desk now.

33

To Live Again

Jerry planned a business trip out of town for a week. I had never taken the children out of school to go home when he was away, but this time I felt certain I should. They were having exams . . . school was almost out. It was May 2, 1973. I didn't understand the urgency of planning a trip home, but I knew I could spend the time in the hospital with Big and maybe help Mother. It would be nice for her to come home from work and find someone there to greet her. Big had broken his hip and was back in the hopsital.

His life was rapidly running out . . . but things were different. I smiled each time I remembered that afternoon in the nursing home just two months ago. We had been telling him good-bye. That was always hard for him and us. Everyone left the room but me, and I called out to them, "Be there in a minute." Big and I were alone. I sat on the edge of his bed. It's now or never, I thought suddenly.

He reached for my hand, and I held his. *Make him able to hear me, God . . . his hearing is so bad . . . and let his mind be clear.*

We looked at each other for a few moments. "Do you need Jesus, yet?" I asked.

The tears rolled down his face and onto his new pajamas. He nodded his head. Through a simple prayer of need and confession, Big became a child of God. Somehow when I got back to the car, Jerry and Mother knew what had happened, and I knew they knew. We rejoiced silently; we would talk about it later . . . not now.

I would like spending time with Big at the hospital. Mother had told him I was coming. She told me he had said, "Thank God."

I remembered the last thing he'd said to me on our most recent visit. He had seen me look at him and the suffering he was enduring must have reflected in my face. I didn't always remember to smile like my mother did. He reached up and grabbed my hand with strength that amazed me and said in a hoarse whisper, "It's all right . . . now." Big never beat around the bush about anything. He meant it. He was ready to die now. Fear had been removed. He even wanted to talk about who he'd see in heaven, and we spent much time talking about the people, calling them by name, that we thought he'd see. He smiled and named many old friends he wanted to "look up."

I got to Elberton around four in the afternoon. I hadn't hurried. We had stopped by Athens to see Hilda and Grace and others. "How's Big?" they asked. "About the same." I didn't know he had suffered a stroke twenty-four hours earlier, and Mother had decided not to tell me. She knew I would soon be there.

I went to the hospital first. A friend, Louise Bell, sat with Big. Her eyes warned me, "You can't communicate with him," but I ignored her look and sat on the bed.

"Big. Big . . ."

His eyes were open, but there was no gleam of life in them. No response at all. I watched him breathing slowly and with difficulty . . . and stroked his white hair, "Do you want anything?"

"He's trying to say something," Louise cried softly.

And then slowly, from one eye, the one that was not paralyzed from the stroke, tears streamed. They formed little puddles in the hollows under his eyes and in his cheek. I wiped them away over and over. Then I kissed him good-bye and said, "I'll see you later, okay?"

Mother and I came back after she got off from work. She still hadn't missed working. We looked at him silently, and the doctor came in and insisted she go home. I was relieved when she agreed. We drove home heavy-hearted, but she smiled a lot. She talked about the funeral. "I want a white cross on the casket. That's all. No flowers, and I want someone to read, not sing, "Near The Cross."

I nodded in agreement, wondering how it was possible that we were talking about this so calmly, but grateful that we could. She wanted my approval. I gave it.

We undressed for bed. I carefully laid my clothes out. I expected to have to put them back on in a hurry. I got in bed feeling strange . . . like being homesick when I was a little girl. *Thank you, Lord, that I'm here in Elberton. Your timing is perfect.* I had prayed for two years that I would already be here when Big's time came. I wanted to be the one to answer the phone and tell my mother. I didn't want her to have to call me.

I prayed for about thirty minutes. *Take him, Lord. Please take him now. His life is over. Take him to be with you. I give him up, and I know my mother does, too.*

I answered the phone on the first hint of a ring. It was nearly eleven. "Thank you, Louise. We'll be right there. Mother, let's go. It was the hospital." But she was already up and dressing. Jerry's father came and got Jennifer and Jeremy. The other two children were already with them. I had a feeling of peace as we drove to the hospital.

I knew by the way Louise looked when we got off the elevator that he was gone . . . but we went to his room, like we had so many times before. The sheets were wrinkled and he was lying like a baby, curled up . . . and I thought, he's going to move. I know he is. Nothing can be this still. My mother accepted death immediately and said softly, "All right, darling," and kissed his forehead. I touched his hand. It was warm. Memories of the things I had seen his hands do flashed through my mind . . . plant a dogwood tree, dress a fish, build a stand for a Christmas tree, sooth one of my children's hurts, stir his morning coffee . . .

I would have stayed, transfixed by the incredible stillness, if my mother hadn't touched me and said, "Let's go."

Jerry came in the next day from his meeting. I called Venera and asked for her prayers. The funeral was May 4. He had missed living to be eighty-five by four days.

I lifted Jeremy up to the casket, praying, "Help him, dear God, he's so little. Help him to understand death." Jeremy smiled down at him, then looked at me. "This is his old body, Mama. His new one's in heaven with Jesus . . . and his foot don't hurt no more."

That terrible pain that I expected never came, and I stopped looking for it. But even now when I see someone that looks like Big or moves like him, my heart quickens. I watched an elderly man getting his morning paper as I was driving carpool, and I remembered Big so clearly. He loved the early morning, especially in the spring.

A man shuffling along in the grocery store startled me one day as I rounded a corner, and I stood motionless staring at him. "Hello," he smiled, his blue eyes twinkling.

"Hi," I smiled at him in fascination. I guess he wondered why my eyes filled with tears as we spoke.

A large display of sorghum syrup was in my path. I stopped and looked at it, remembering Big on a winter's morning preparing his syrup biscuit. He could make it look unbelievably good, and I didn't even like breakfast, much less sorghum syrup. But I tossed a bottle of it in my grocery cart.

I had given him a yellow rose on his last birthday. I remembered, how, sitting in a chair, he tended it. The rose bush thrived. He could make anything grow. But it seemed to fade after he went to the hospital the last time. By the time Big left us the rose was a dead stob in the ground. But my mother kept working with it, and one day when we visited her, I saw that a tiny green sprout had come out on it.

Now it blooms radiantly again, and each time I see it I am reminded that Big lives again, also.

34

What's Tongue Therapy?

When Dr. Robert Lahr told me matter of factly that he wanted Julie to finish up her orthodontic work with tongue therapy lessons,

I thought that sounds ridiculous. He must be teasing. What's tongue therapy?

But I told him I would make the appointment with the tongue therapist, Mrs. Stewart. The idea of exercising one's tongue to prevent teeth from becoming crooked again didn't seem reasonable to me. But I trusted Dr. Lahr. Not only because his treatment for our girls had achieved remarkable results in a short period of time, but because he was a Christian. He shared the "Four Spiritual Laws" with each of his patients as routinely as he said, "Open wide." The first time I went into his examining room I was surprised and pleased to see the neat stack of small, yellow booklets explaining the plan of salvation on his dental tray.

I remembered when Dr. Lahr had announced to Jerry and me that both Julie and Jennifer needed braces, I nearly fell off the little stool I was sitting on. How would we afford it? How would I manage to drive across Atlanta in the traffic? How would I ever find the office again?

Jerry had told him immediately to go ahead with the braces for both girls . . . and looked at me as if to indicate: "Don't say we can't afford it. Teeth are important. I'll handle this."

I looked away, glad he was so sure this was right. I wasn't. Julie and Jennifer knew I was worried as we drove home. "Mama, you're always telling us to give God all our worries. You aren't giving this to him. You're worrying," Jennifer said.

"Yeah," Julie agreed, "Give it up, Mama."

They're right, God. I must give this to you.

And I did it driving home that day. The financial problems I had feared just didn't develop. Many of our monthly bills were reduced to only one third of what I'd expected because Dr. Lahr didn't need to adjust their braces often. Julie was out of hers in an amazing five months and wore only a mouthpiece.

The traffic problems actually helped me learn to drive in Atlanta with more confidence. We often prayed at a particular traffic light . . . and someone always let me turn.

But, just when I thought Julie's treatment was complete, there was something called tongue therapy. Mrs. Stewart gave the lessons at Dr. Lahr's office.

I brought Julie for her first lesson and was keenly aware of my ugly attitude. *Well, Lord, I'm going to claim Romans 8:28 again. "And we know that all that happens to us is working for our good if we love God and are fitting into his plan"* (TLB). *I can't imagine how you will work something good out of this for me, but I'm trusting you to do it.*

Right away I felt better and looked around in the waiting room for someone to talk with. Everyone was reading. There was always good literature in Dr. Lahr's office, but I felt like talking today. Just then a mother came in with teenage identical twin sons. Mothers of twins share a bond that doesn't call for introductions. I began talking immediately to her. She was friendly, and we compared experiences of raising twins. She had five children. I admired her calm manner and happy attitude and the fact her hair was in curlers, and she never referred to it.

"Are you waiting here or shopping?" she asked.

"I don't know my way around well enough to shop. I'll have to wait here," I said. But I had the delicious feeling she was going to ask me to go with her.

"Want to go to a book store with me?"

"Oh yes." *Wonderful . . . a book store. She could have asked me to go to a material shop with her. I hated those.*

We started talking about books and Christianity. She was easy to talk with and didn't look at me in a funny, surprised way when I told her I liked to write. Most people seemed almost depressed when I mentioned writing and said, "I can't even write letters."

"I'm trying to write a book," I blurted out. I might never see Evelyn Campbell again, so I wanted to talk about writing as much as possible. She was a good listener.

"Wonderful," she smiled and looked over at me for a moment as she drove. She told me she had done some editing, and I knew from our easy conversation about Christianity that she was a Christian.

Talking to her made me feel like I could write a book. I hoped, somehow, I would see her again.

115

The next morning the phone rang early.

"Hello."

"Mrs. West. This is Suzanne Stewart, Julie's tongue therapy teacher. I'm not calling about Julie. I understand you like to write."

How does she know that, Lord? Oh, Evelyn . . . Evelyn Campbell, the mother of twins . . . she must have told her yesterday after I left . . . but why?

"Oh, yes, I do."

"Well, I belong to a small group of writers . . . Christian writers. I think you'd like the group. Will you join us?"

I pushed aside the immediate thoughts of: "They're professionals; you're going to be out of place. You don't know anything about these people . . . maybe they just dabble in religion, and there's probably an enormous fee involved, and you'll have to take a correspondence course. You're not a joiner . . . never were."

And savored the thought, maybe it is exactly what she says and they will help me.

"Yes, yes, I would."

I circled June 23, on my calendar and wrote in large letters "Scribe Tribe meets." Then I opened my Bible praying, "Give me a hint, Lord. Is this from you? Do you want me to write?"

I looked at the page and read, "My word shall be published throughout the land" (Acts 13:49).

I was going to meet writers . . . Christian writers. I made unnecessary trips to the kitchen just to look at what I'd written on my calendar and to remind myself this wasn't a daydream . . . it was real.

35

Meeting the Scribe Tribe

In a couple of days, Cec Murphey, a member of the Scribe Tribe, called to tell me a little about the group and its members. Some of them were professional and published, others beginners like me. He talked about writing and the Lord with a dedication that made me instantly comfortable talking with him.

Cec had told me that he and Mary Jepson and Suzanne were working on entries for the *Guideposts* contest. I couldn't believe I was really going to meet people who were entering the same writing contest as I was. I worked on my manuscript until I thought it was perfect. Then I sent a copy to each member in the group from a list Cec had sent me. Mine would be "critiqued" along with others at the meeting.

Finally the twenty-third arrived. I cooked an especially good supper so Jerry and the children wouldn't think I was neglecting them. I was much too excited to eat.

I arrived at Mary's house twenty minutes early. A large dog and two little boys greeted me. Then Mary and I introduced ourselves to each other and left to pick up Suzanne.

Suzanne dashed out to the car breathlessly in a matching pink shorts and top . . . and I reminded myself that I didn't have any shorts and tops that really matched. And she was late! She hadn't even started getting ready. I had been getting ready all day. She laughed about being late, and I felt even more insecure. I could never be late for anything . . . ever.

Once the three of us were on our way to the meeting, Suzanne and Mary talked about people and things that were strange to me, and I began to wish I hadn't come. Then Suzanne mentioned something the Lord had worked out for her. She smiled a unique smile and looked just like June Allison. Her eyes were inverted U's. Once again, I was glad I had come.

We were meeting at Charlotte Hale Smith's. I knew she was a successful writer. Though I was dying to meet her, I was apprehensive, too. She opened the door to her apartment and even before we were introduced, her eyes insisted, "I'm glad you came."

I looked at her apartment done in greens and blues. I knew she lived alone. What would it be like to be able to write all day in this quiet, lovely place with no interruptions?

The rest of the group arrived, and soon they were critiquing an article. Boy, I thought, Are they ever rough! I don't think I'll come back.

Finally they got to mine. They had saved it until last. Right away everything they said hurt . . . I had tried to get ready, but I never got ready enough.

It was like seven tennis balls coming towards me at once . . . and each one hurt. I had thought my article was nearly perfect. They tore it apart. Suzanne took off her glasses and told me how many *I's* I had on the first page. Mary kept reminding me not to use the verb *to be*. Cec's wife, Shirley, caught each misspelled word. Cec backed up her criticism, "Use your dictionary." I felt like if I had one right then, I would have thrown it at him, but I smiled and nodded mutely.

"Your sentences are too long," someone offered.

"Your real beginning is on the second page," was flung at me.

And improper sentence structure gave a very serious sentence a comical effect, and everyone laughed . . . except me.

How wonderful it would be to get up and run out, but I sat there frozen in my seat, hoping I was still smiling. I made notes furiously.

Oh, finally it was over. I was at home, and I could stop smiling. A mountain of tears rose deep inside me. That hurt, I told myself. Another voice interrupted, "So it hurt. You want to write, don't you?"

"Of course, but how do I get past this pain?"

Still hurting, I prayed, "Lord, thank you for this help with my writing. I've prayed so long for help. Now I have it, and they're good, plenty good, and all I can think about is how much it hurts. Help me get past this hurt. What's the matter with me?"

You've taken your eyes off me. You're looking at yourself.

You're right. I have to get my eyes back on you. Help me.

But the next morning I still hurt, and I wouldn't go near the typewriter. At least not for an hour or two!

By noon I was rewriting the article mentally. Then I could stand it no longer. I got my article out and the notes I'd taken during the meeting, rolling paper into my typewriter.

118

I lost track of time. Hours flew by. I felt like I was learning a new language. A revelation dawned on me. Writing was work. Not a talent, or a gift, althought that might help. But writing was work . . . maybe the hardest in the world.

Are you willing to work at it?

Yes. I just didn't know work was involved, Lord. I really thought it was just supposed to flow out.

I felt like God smiled at my discovery. I went out and bought a new typewriter ribbon, a dictionary, and an eraser.

Then I started working on my article again. Now as I typed, the Scribe Tribe seemed to lean over my shoulder.

"That's a new paragraph."

"Don't use *was*."

"How did you really feel?"

"That insults my intelligence."

"Look it up."

I had my final copy. I decided to take it to Suzanne and *if* she didn't look too busy and *if* she smiled her June Allison smile, I would ask her to read it.

"Would you have time to read this and mail it back to me?" I asked her.

She smiled like June Allison again and said, "I'll read it now."

She read slowly, and I looked out the window.

"This is beautiful." She wiped tears from her eyes.

I floated out of the office.

Thank you Lord for these wonderful people you've led me to because Julie required tongue therapy.

36

And the Winner Is . . .

I knew it wasn't an accident that I had become part of the Scribe Tribe. I wrote to Grace, Hilda, Bobby, and others, telling them about my writing group and the contest.

Jerry's mother offered to keep our children if I won the *Guideposts'* contest. Jerry said I could go.

The four of us in the writing group put our entries in the mail. We felt that surely one of us would win . . . and I thought, it just might be me.

We had to wait thirty days to learn who the winners were. There would be twenty selected in the United States. And I thought more and more that I would be one of the twenty.

I spent a lot of time writing and many of my articles were being accepted. *Home Life* accepted nearly everything I sent them.

One day I prayed, "Lord, I need a larger desk."

Yes, you do.

Where will I find a desk?

There are plenty available. Look. There's one for you.

I decided to enjoy my hobby of reading the want ads. Under *Office Furniture, Used,* I saw an ad by a business that had six desks for sale. When I called, the manager told me they were going fast. He was only asking thirty-five dollars for each of them. I knew I couldn't drive to downtown Atlanta to get it.

That night I asked Jerry: "Would you look at a desk for me tomorrow? I really need one, and we have space in the den. I have the money from an article I sold. If you think it looks okay, get it for me. Would you?"

To my delight, he wrote the address down, took my check, and said he'd look if he had time and remembered.

Please, Lord, save one for me and let Jerry remember to go.

It was after two the next day when I saw a truck turning into our street, and Jerry was driving it! He looked pleased. Even before the truck stopped I saw part of my desk on the back of the truck. Jerry got out, "It doesn't look too great. You may not even want it. It was the only one they had left."

I nodded, already loving the desk . . . and Jerry for driving forty miles during his lunch hour.

The desk seemed enormous. 5½ by 2½ feet. It even had a place for a typewriter.

Thirty days passed. Charlotte, who had won a *Guideposts'* writing contest and knew the staff and contest procedure, said it was a good indication they were still considering our manuscripts since we hadn't gotten them back. "Maybe we'll all win," we laughed.

Mary's came back, then Suzanne's. Finally Cec's. But not mine.

Lord, you're going to have to help me over this fear of flying I have because it looks like I'm going to be flying to New York.

Even Jerry asked if I'd heard anything from *Guideposts*. I waited for the mailman every day and told people that knew I'd entered the contest: "I'm willing to do whatever God wants. It's all right if I don't win. He just has something else for me."

It sure sounded "spiritual," but I didn't mean it. I wanted to be a winner. I *had* to be a winner. I thought about it continually, imagining how I would find the letter in the mailbox and run tell my family and call members of the Scribe Tribe. Then I would probably buy a new dress. It was going to be wonderful . . . Cinderella had nothing on me.

One morning I didn't feel well. By that night I had a high fever. The next day the pain in my back made moving almost impossible. Jerry's parents came over and took the children home with them. Jerry took me to the doctor. He said it was a severe virus that made you think you were dying. "Right," I agreed weakly.

He prescribed more rest and said the children should remain with their grandparents a day or two more. I thought it was excellent advice. The next morning I felt better, but was weak and stayed in bed. I was bored and imagined winning the contest some more.

Then a question zoomed in: *Why do you tell people you've given this up?*

Well, Lord, it must be your will for me to go. You put me with these people who can write just when I was working on my entry. Your timing is always perfect.

So is my will. Give it up.

I can accept losing.

Can you?

I don't want to think about it.

You must. You haven't been honest with your friends, yourself,

121

or me. *You're holding onto winning.*

Tears streamed down my face. *I know. I want it so much. Please, let me win. Let me go. I'll work hard . . . harder than anyone there. I have to go.*

Give it up.

I can't. I can't. I want to, but I can't. Help me.

By that afternoon I was feeling well enough to get up. That afternoon I stopped by Venera's and as I started out I asked, "Got anything good to read?"

"Have you read this?" She handed me a book.

It was *My Burden Is Light* by Eugenia Price.

Halfway through the book I knew God meant me to have that book at this particular time. Early the next morning I got up and read alone at my kitchen table. I finished the book, sobbing softly. "Thank you, Lord. Thank you for using this book to help me give up winning. I'm ready to know now that I'm not the winner. Thank you for teaching me so patiently."

A few hours later the mailman brought my returned article. I was able to open it and smile, feeling no disappointment . . . only joy that God was working in my life and had prepared me for this. I told the girls, and they looked as if they might cry. "Have you told Daddy?" Jennifer whispered.

"No. I'll tell him sometime," I smiled. But Jennifer ran up the stairs. It was Saturday and Jerry was at home. She ran back to me, like a little messenger: "Mama, Daddy is really sorry . . . he looked so disappointed. I'm sorry too, Mama. I prayed for you to win."

"I learned how to lose, Jen. God never intended me to win this contest." I smiled and she knew I meant it.

37

Fireworks

Home Life had accepted nine of my articles and the editor, George Knight, had written me several warm, lengthy letters. He did return one article and wrote, "You are long overdue a rejection!" I laughed and then was amazed at myself—laughing about a rejection.

Now I knew I must get on with the writing of my book. I got the first three chapters ready for the writing group and was nearly as scared as the first time I went. This book was different from anything I'd ever submitted. it was the inside of my heart. They saved mine until last. No one said much of anything. Cec told me I still couldn't spell. It was a joke in the group. I was officially the worst speller. "But you can write," they agreed, encouraging me. The same thing my English professor had told me twenty years before. I thought about how he encouraged me, and I wrote him a belated thank-you note. I heard from him shortly. He expressed delight at hearing from me after twenty years and learning that his teaching had some effect on my life. Then he added: "You are improving. Only two misspelled words. Hang in there!" When I read the last part of Dr. Walker's letter, the Scribe Tribe shouted with laughter.

But now they weren't saying much of anything. *Lord, I need some encouragement.*

Charlotte spoke softly and with assurance, it seemed to me. She sounded like Bobby Leverett. "This book is going to make it."

Joy exploded in my heart. I felt both gratitude and embarrassment.

The next day I wrote seven hours straight, ignoring anything or anybody that tried to stop me. Even though I was exhausted, I couldn't leave the typewriter. I tried. I couldn't. For three days I wrote like this, not even realizing what day or month it was.

Jerry gave me a look that said: "This is enough of this. You can work sensibly." I knew he was right, but it didn't matter. I was like a snowball rolling down a hill.

I wrote nearly half the book in those three days. Then I got up and called Charlotte.

"Give me a lecture, Charlotte. Writing is devouring me, and I'm pushing away from my family, friends, even the church."

Charlotte's words soothed me like ointment on a burn. She had been where I was and understood. God gave her the words I needed to hear. I was finally able to ask God to help me slow down. I must learn patience, I thought. I must.

As I worked on the book, the phone interrupted one day.

"This is George Knight of *Home Life* magazine," an unfamiliar voice said. Speechless, I tingled with goose flesh. I had often imagined an editor calling me for something . . . anything. What a thrill it would be!

"George Knight, ahh, ahh," I stammered, "Really George Knight. Oh me, I can't think of anything to say. I'll think of something after we hang up." His instant laughter made me comfortable. He talked about my writing, and he reminded me how many of my articles they had accepted.

Maybe he wants me to stop sending them so much material, my mind raced ahead. No, he wouldn't call for that.

What does he want, Lord?

Listen. You are always so impatient.

"We at *Home Life* want you to come to Nashville and attend a writer's workshop and accept a writing assignment. We believe you are ready."

Oh, Lord. Do you hear? A writer's conference . . . after I gave up the one at Guideposts. *Do you hear?*

Do I hear? I planned this. It is my way. The other was YOUR *way.*

"I want to, Mr. Knight. Let me check with Jerry."

"Good. We'll fly you up, of course."

Oh, Lord. I can't fly. I thought I could, but I'm afraid. You know I can't fly.

"Could Jerry drive me, Mr. Knight?"

"Of course. Call me back in three days with your decision and remember me to Jerry and all the children."

I hung up the phone and walked to the window. The sky should be filled with fireworks or something. But everything looked just the same. The children played. Julie was sun bathing. The dog slept in the shade. A car drove by.

Well, never mind, I can feel the fireworks. They are in my heart.

124

38

No Way Around

I'm going with you on the flight to Nashville, a patient, loving voice insisted. *I'm going to dissolve your fear of flying.*

Jeremy prayed I wouldn't be afraid. His faith often amazed me. It had touched me deeply one evening at the spring revival. Jerry was out of town, and the children and I were attending. Suddenly I knew God was telling me something.

I'm going to call Jeremy tonight. Don't worry about him being only six. Don't think about people criticizing his age. Don't go with him. Just give him your blessings. That's all you are to do. Look at him now. See. He's already responding.

Tears filled my eyes as I looked over at him. Sitting on the edge of the pew, his feet not touching the floor. A hole in his shoes. He needed a haircut. A scratch on his elbow. He sat motionless, listening to the visiting minister, Bill Sauer, as if he were Popeye.

What about Jon, Lord? He will want to go, too.

Just then Jon put his head down in my lap and shut his eyes. He had gone to sleep in church only three times in his life. Usually he couldn't sit still long enough to go to sleep.

Everyone stood up to sing the hymn of invitation. I sat with Jon sleeping in my lap. As we sang the last stanza Jeremy came over to me. Tears streamed down his face. He put his head on my shoulder and his arms around my neck. My tears fell onto his head. "It's all right," I whispered. He bolted down the aisle and joined the others who had responded and stood straight and tall like a little soldier.

Venera was a counselor, and she talked with him and gave him a book about growing with Jesus. He handed it to me when he joined me again and said, "I can't read. Help me study about Jesus."

Some of my closest friends came up to speak to me—only words weren't necessary. They just reached out and touched my hand.

Jon woke up and was happy over Jeremy's decision. Jeremy told me the next day he didn't think it was time for him to be baptized yet, but he would know when the time was. I agreed with him. We began studying the book together, and he answered many of the questions about trust with amazing simplicity.

A few days after his decision, he made a little wooden cross from two sticks and held it together with a rubber band. He sat it on his dresser. I picked it up one day and held it, remembering the wooden cross at Beech Haven that I couldn't understand . . . that I didn't even want to look at.

I still didn't fully understand the cross, and probably never would, but I knew now that back then I had been trying to circumvent it.

39

The Right Neighbor

I accepted the fact that I would fly to Nashville. I even laughed thinking about it . . . maybe I'll write an article called "Up, Up, and Afraid." Then I prayed, "I'm trusting you, Lord. The worst thing that can happen is to die, and that is not nearly as frightening . . . as just being afraid. I'm going to fly and trust you." I knew flying was God's way. Jerry's taking me had been *my* way. Would I ever stop trying to do things my way?

Sitting out in the yard one day, I noticed a neighbor coming over. It felt good to see her coming over, for no special reason . . . just to chat, like Hilda and I used to.

Pat was younger than I, but very friendly and we had children the same age. I had invited her to several spiritual events, but she declined politely. I began praying for her. She just seemed to pop into my prayers.

For the two years we had been in Lilburn, I had longed for a special spiritual neighbor to share with. I loved the running-back-and-forth type of sharing. I had prayed for two years that the lot next to me would be bought and a house built on it. I really felt

God was going to give me this special neighbor and I started thanking him for her, whoever she was.

But the lot remained for sale, and I didn't understand why my "right" neighbor didn't appear.

Pat sat down in a lawn chair, and suddenly we were talking about Jesus. She was excited as we talked. It wasn't the polite type of conversation we had when I asked her to attend spiritual events with me. I asked her to attend a Bible study on Friday. Tricia was teaching here for six weeks at Frances Bowen's. I had asked Pat to go to earlier studies when Tricia had first begun the course, but she couldn't or didn't want to. I wasn't sure which. But when I asked her this time, she said, "Yes, I want to go."

And then she went to the last meeting with me. I took the first four chapters of "Out of My Bondage" with me to let Tricia read. Pat started reading it as we drove to the Bible study. "Marion," she gasped, "I didn't know anyone else ever felt like this but me."

She had no idea how much what she said meant to me. Through my book I wanted to communicate with mothers . . . and I had just reached my first.

Pat prayed to receive Christ that day. She told me about it. But she didn't really have to. I saw it in her face . . . she was glowing.

Slowly it dawned on me. *Lord, Pat is my neighbor I have been asking you to send me for two years. She has been here all the time. Will I ever stop doing things my way?*

40

Freed from Bondage

Today as I dusted my white bowl and pitcher, I ran my hand over the crack that was barely visible. I smiled remembering the night just recently when Jerry had broken it. I had screamed, "Oh no!" It had been Big's, and I loved it dearly.

That night in bed Jerry asked in the darkness, "Are you mad?"

"About what?"

"The bowl. I'm sorry. I know how much it meant to you."

Incredible! I had forgotten about it. "No, I'm not mad, really."

"I got some glue while I was out tonight. We'll glue it back together, no matter how long it takes."

"Thanks." I lay there in the darkness thinking how I had forgotten about the broken bowl . . . and instantly forgiven Jerry. I was filled with love for him as I thought about his buying the glue.

This type of forgiveness—this type of life—had been available all along . . . and I nearly missed it. I remembered the fights we'd had about things like my not getting all the strings off the green beans; not matching his socks when I put them in his drawer; his forgetting to mail my letters; my inability to balance the checkbook . . . and my having to wait for him on Sunday mornings to go to Sunday School—all those fusses had been unnecessary.

I can't yet say that I *always* like not having things *my* way, but I believe that if I stay teachable, God will continue to help me . . . day by day, moment by moment. Jesus told us about this way of living when he said he came that we might have life and have it *more abundantly.*

Loading the dishwasher after supper tonight, I thought about the trip to Nashville as I heard a plane roar overhead. *I was really going to fly, despite my great fear of flying . . . and accept my first writing assignment.* Joy overflowed in my heart.

Pat seemed to walk through my mind . . . my "right neighbor." I was enjoying the flow of happy thoughts when suddenly I thought: *Does Jerry have a shirt ironed for tomorrow?* Before I could go and check, I heard our garbage cans rattling. I ran outside hoping to prevent a dog from turning them over. I was too late.

I picked up the trash and began replacing it in the can. A breeze tiptoed by, carrying the sweet smell of honeysuckle. Crickets sang their night songs in syncopated rhythm. I stood still in the moonlight and gazed up at the sky. Orion had never shone more beautifully.

I knew that God had reached down and touched me . . . and set me free.

Smiling, I hurried back inside.

128